TREK

VS.
THE NEXT
GENERATION

JAMES VAN HISE

COVER ART BY MORRIS SCOTT DOLLENS

Library of Congress Cataloging-in-Publication Data
James Van Hise, 1959—

    Trek Vs. The Next Generation

    1. Trek Vs. The Next Generation (television, popular culture)
I. Title

Published by Pioneer Books, Inc., 5715 N. Balsam Rd., Las Vegas, NV, 89130.

First Printing, 1993

Publisher and Designer: Hal Schuster   *Editor: David Lessnick*

CONTENTS

DEDICATION

TO

Dreamers

TREK

VS.

THE NEXT GENERATION

THE CLASSIC TREK CAST AND THE CAST OF THE NEXT GENERATION MEET ON JUNE 6, 1991 AT PARAMOUNT STUDIOS.

INTRODUCTION
AND THE WINNER IS . . .

While some fans still adopt an "Us vs. Them" approach to the STAR TREK vs. THE NEXT GENERATION question, many others have accepted the fact that it's all part of the same universe. THE NEXT GENERATION is a linear spin-off of Classic Trek. It follows the adventures of the U.S.S. Enterprise further into the future, showing ahow the pressures of the passage of time and the mechanizations of interstellar politics have changed some things for better or worse. But it's all STAR TREK.

Gene Roddenberry had a vision for future humanity and that's what STAR TREK is about. It is about a belief in a future where optimism can be practiced. In spite of the problems the crew of the Enterprise encounter on a weekly basis, it is still a bright future. The seemingly insurmountable problems of the late 20th century didn't hold us back after all. Roddenberry insisted that this would be true. It's this underlying optimism which forms the basis of STAR TREK. This is why an episode like "Yesterday's Enterprise" is so startling because instead of having an underlying optimism, the story has an underlying fatalism as the Federation is on the verge of losing a brutal 20 year war to the Klingons. In Gene Roddenberry's dream world there is always a light at the end of the tunnel.

Trek Classic and THE NEXT GENERATION have more similarities than differences. This book explores the many aspects of both. From the characters, to the stories, to the technology common to both series. It's all STAR TREK, both good and bad. Is there a clear winner?

—JAMES VAN HISE

LEONARD NIMOY AND WILLIAM SHATNER ON MARCH 28, 1978 AT THE STAR TREK PRESS CONFERENCE AT PARAMOUNT STUDIOS.

CHAPTER 1
TREK CLASSIC:
Shaping the Dream

In the beginning there was Kirk, Spock, McCoy and the man who created them, Gene Roddenberry. But was STAR TREK originally created as a product of the times or a true reflection of a growing interest in things to come?

To a child of the sixties, STAR TREK was very much a part of life. We grew up with it and we read everything we could about the show. After all, science fiction on television was rare in those days. And someone writing about it was even more rare, particularly when the articles contained some solid information.

Initially all we knew about this new show was what we read. Would the show live up to the hype? In those days hype about television shows was in its relative infancy and articles in magazines and newspapers tended to strive to give us "just the facts," as another sixties TV series often said.

In an article which appeared in the BUFFALO EVENING NEWS from September 3, 1966, we were introduced to the series which was set to premiere a few days later.

The article began: "A 400-man space ship, the U.S.S. Enterprise, cruises the TV universe this fall starting Thursday night in STAR TREK, NBC's expensive full-hour science fiction adventure series about puny man exploring the wild blue yonder." But then every science fiction series is referred to as being "expensive." Sometimes it's even true.

"Starring the talented Canadian actor William Shatner as space ship commander Kirk, assisted by brainy, elf-eared Mr. Spock (Leonard Nimoy), STAR TREK goes back and forth in time, jousting with alien spirits, bewildering viruses and ordinary human conflicts on a never-ending trip to other worlds.

"NBC hopes the science-fiction plots won't seem never-ending, and lays stress on the solid adventure approach. 'We're not going to be like the children's show, LOST IN SPACE, where characters battle villains in eerie costumes,' said star Shatner, coming back to earth on a lunch break. 'We deal with human conflicts against a science fiction background.' "

AN EYE ON THE FUTURE

When Gene Roddenberry created STAR TREK, his concept of the five-year mission wasn't just an arbitrary number that he pulled out of the air; he fully expected the series to last at least five years. A series which can last five years is considered a hit with vast syndication potential for a lucrative return. But not even Gene Roddenberry believed in 1966 that STAR TREK would be alive and actively generating new stories and spin-offs nearly 30 years later.

The 1960's were a turbulent time. When Roddenberry originally conceived STAR TREK, it was shortly after the assassination of President Kennedy. The civil rights movement was very active and strife in the United States and was a commonplace event. As though in reaction to that, Roddenberry conceived a future 300 years from now in which humanity had survived those dark days of the 20th century and conquered the stars. It was an optimistic future at a time when few people were optimistic about anything. And by the time STAR TREK was canceled, Robert Kennedy and Martin Luther King had been assassinated as well. But STAR TREK defiantly proclaimed that we would survive these difficult days. The second season episode "Assignment: Earth" even went out of its way to say so.

In the midst of the chaos, Roddenberry believed that mankind would endure. But while many '60s series refused to deal with the turmoil of the time and just ignored it, Roddenberry took the tack of looking beyond it. He recognized that every decade has its seemingly hopeless odds to overcome and if humanity could survive the turmoil of World War II, then it could survive the social upheaval of the '60s as well. It was time to look to the future and not be mired in the problems of the present.

WAGON TRAIN TO THE STARS

Science fiction wasn't exactly a television staple in the early '60s. In order to sell the concept to skeptical network executives, Roddenberry had to cloak it in more familiar terms. The western was still a popular genre so Roddenberry described STAR TREK as "WAGON TRAIN to the stars." WAGON TRAIN was a popular series in the late '50s and early '60s about a group of wagons heading west and the adventures along the way.

The Enterprise became the wagon train, and other worlds were the towns they stopped off at each week. The Klingons and Romulans were stand-ins for Indians. If that sounds like an oversimplification of the show, it is. But that's nevertheless how it was sold. Even LOST IN SPACE was nothing more than an atomic age update of the children's classic SWISS FAMILY ROBINSON (which coincidentally Disney had done as a popular feature film in 1960). So everything old does indeed become new again, one way or another.

When Roddenberry initially began sketching out his ideas for STAR TREK, only Mr. Spock was conceived as being a part of that early premise. Captain Robert T. April was the first commander of the Enterprise, and his name has been used in subsequent STAR TREK adventures, both in novels and in the animated series. People familiar with the first STAR TREK pilot will recognize the names of some of the others: Yeoman J.M. Colt, Dr. Philip Boyce, Jose Tyler and especially Number One. During the script writing stage Robert April was replaced with Christopher Pike.

The Network executives at NBC found "The Cage" interesting, but "too cerebral," a description which will no doubt haunt those unnamed individuals to their grave. But they liked it enough to offer to pay for a second pilot—so long as Roddenberry got rid of that overbearing female, Number One, and that Satanic looking alien named Spock.

STAR TREK—REVISED

Roddenberry found it easier to fight for, and keep, the alien Spock than to keep the woman as second in command. In 1965 men found the concept of taking orders from a woman, much less seeing one treated as an absolute equal, to be a bit too radical. So they let Spock stay.

The cool exterior of Number One was transplanted onto Spock, who was a bit too intense in "The Cage." Even Nimoy has said in recent years that he initially tended to overact when he was starting out and had to learn that there was something to be said for employing restraint in a performance.

What would STAR TREK have been like without Spock? Clearly the character was an important part of the ensemble, and his very presence added vital elements to certain stories. Would STAR TREK have achieved its longevity if Kirk and McCoy were the big two on the series? One can indulge in endless speculation on such an idea.

While the first STAR TREK pilot used Spock as largely just one of several characters (the doctor has more scenes and better dialogue in "The Cage" than Spock does), he was clearly retooled in important ways by the time he was seen in "Where No Man Has Gone Before," the second pilot. When the series went into production, the possibilities evident in Spock were already being explored by Roddenberry and his writing staff.

Within four episodes, the inner turmoil of the character was brought boiling to the surface in "The Naked Time." Spock revealed in that episode to his captain that, "I couldn't even tell my mother that I loved her." And more directly to Kirk himself, "When I feel friendship for you, I am ashamed." Spock as the outsider and the outcast was born, and even though he never bared his soul in such a manner again, the viewers never forgot. The cold, cool exterior of the Vulcan was a mask. He wasn't such an alien figure after all, in spite of those pointed ears. He was as torn up inside about how he fit into the world around him as many others were who watched that show. It was inevitable that a vast following would build up around the character overnight.

THE NEW MAN IN CHARGE

In "The Cage," we see a commander of the Enterprise who is much different from James T. Kirk. Captain Pike, played by Jeffrey Hunter, finds the responsibilities of command a heavy burden to bear—so heavy that he is seriously considering resigning his commission and leaving Starfleet. What bothers him is that any decision he makes on an almost daily basis could result in the death of one of his crew, and he recently saw just that happen. Pike just didn't want to be responsible for any more lives, or deaths.

He was as remote and aloof from his crew as Number One was, perhaps because he didn't want to take the chance of getting close to someone who would not survive his command. When Pike unburdens himself to Dr. Boyce, it is only because he is considering leaving Starfleet and he needs to tell someone how angry he is over the needless deaths he'd recently witnessed and how he should have anticipated trouble. Dr. Boyce's diagnosis is that Pike needs a vacation—a relief from duty, which in a bizarre way the captain gets on planet Talos IV.

On the other hand, in the second pilot, "Where No Man Has Gone Before," William Shatner portrayed Captain Kirk as a commander who took his command no less seriously than Pike, but who did not let it weigh on him. He faced the hard choices and he made them, even when it involved Gary Mitchell, one of his oldest friends. When STAR TREK was picked up as a series, DeForest Kelley became the new ship's doctor. His addition to the cast created a three-part chemistry between Kirk, Spock and McCoy, something which is difficult to achieve in an ongoing series.

THE BIG THREE

This chemistry contributed to the reasons why the series still holds up under repeated viewings. Even when we know exactly what's going to happen, watching the interaction among the three stars makes for highly entertaining viewing. The three personalities are very different and yet they managed to compliment one another in the way they work together.

When you have three characters who function so well together, it opens up many possibilities for the writers to explore. Kirk is the decisive commander. Spock's cool logic points out the unpleasant necessities while McCoy challenges these decisions based on their human cost. And yet these three are friends. They are just three very different people. It wasn't long before entire episodes were spun around stories involving just these three characters, virtually to the exclusion of most all of the others. This is particularly true of "The City On The Edge Of Forever," "Mirror, Mirror," "Mantrap" and "Miri" to name a few.

PERFECT SCIENCE FICTION FORMAT

STAR TREK was the first science fiction series with continuing characters that adults could relate to. There were certain setbacks, and even Roddenberry later acknowledged that the Klingons were pretty much cartoon bad guys with no redeeming characteristics. Majel Barrett stated that Gene actually came to hate the Klingons because of the simplistic approach taken with them. When Roddenberry had the opportunity to set this matter right in THE NEXT GENERATION, he actually made the Klingons some of the most interesting and complicated characters in the STAR TREK universe. In his own eyes he had redeemed himself.

The restrictions STAR TREK worked under came from the fact that the network couldn't imagine that the average TV viewer would find very much to relate to in a series about people living 300 years in the future on a spaceship. They initially resisted Spock right up to the wire. When brochures were sent out to the network affiliates announcing the series, a photo of Spock had been altered to eliminate the points on his ears and thereby head off any possible backlash from their affiliate stations.

The affiliates are those stations which carry the network shows in each city. They are regarded as vitally important as an affiliate could refuse to carry a show if they felt that showing it would reflect badly on them. Thankfully STAR TREK didn't encounter this, in spite of the supposedly "Satanic" looking Mr. Spock.

In 1966, in spite of the fact that NASA and the space program were very much in the news, the networks couldn't see the correlation between contemporary space launches and TV shows which projected where that technology could lead a couple hundred years from now. In July 1969 when Neal Armstrong walked on the Moon, viewers all across the globe witnessed the event on their TV sets, but by then STAR TREK had already been canceled. The network just didn't get it.

And yet there was a large audience ready to see what the future of our descendants in space might be like. We wanted to know what the relatively primitive spacecraft technology of the 1960's could evolve into. STAR TREK showed us that and answered many other questions along those lines. Aliens in space? But of course. In fact they'll be working alongside of us like it's the most natural thing in the world, just like inter-racial harmony is.

COLORFUL IDEAS

STAR TREK developed a loyal following right from the start because it was both different and accessible. Like THE TWILIGHT ZONE before it, the series told parables and morality tales, but it never forgot to be an action/adventure show. "City On The Edge of Forever" told a story of timecrossed lovers, although its effect has been diluted somewhat by the fact that Kirk had subsequent unhappy love affairs. Still, who can forget that ending in which Kirk ignores the invitation of The Guardian to travel in time again as the captain states, "Let's get the Hell out of here." Author Peter David even used this scene as a jumping off point in IMZADI, one of his recent NEXT GENERATION novels published by Pocket Books.

In episodes such as that one, "This Side of Paradise" and others, STAR TREK produced scripts equal with the best which was being nominated for Emmy Awards in televised drama at the time, but science fiction was never considered for such an honor in the sixties. While the Writer's Guild of America chose science fiction scripts from its members at the time to bestow awards on, the Television Academy didn't follow suit.

In the sixties, not only was color television quite new (1966 marked only the second year in which all new TV series were filmed in color), but it was approached very consciously. The TV costumes were essentially so colorful because it made the entire show look more colorful. The cinematographer, Jerry Finnerman, even lit scenes with colored gels over lights which shown on the walls in the background of sets so that off-white walls could be made to appear red, blue or green. Even now one can watch an episode of the original STAR TREK and see how different it looks visually from any of the TV shows being done today.

The use of colors in this was also logical from the viewpoint of the show's internal logic. Traveling in space for prolonged periods could easily become dull unless the ship was designed in such a way that boredom could be lessened. It made everything more appealing to the eye. The dramatic impact of this is particularly effective when an episode of Trek Classic is seen on a big screen, such as at a convention. The effect is similar to watching an early Technicolor motion picture from the '30s and '40s where color was regarded as just as important an element of the total motion picture experience as the actors and the script are.

MODERN REVISIONISM

In the modern motion picture revivals, this has been peculiarly lacking. Robert Wise was even quoted as stating that he chose the pastel colors for uniforms in STAR TREK—THE MOTION PICTURE because he felt that the colors on the TV show would have been too garish for a big screen film. Clearly the opposite was the case. The drab costumes used in the first motion picture detracted from the viewing experience and made the colorful special effects even more dynamic in contrast. But then the '60s was a time when bright colors were the order of the day while in the '70s styles had changed, and this has apparently been reflected in the motion pictures as well.

Another major difference between Trek Classic and its modern off-shoots can be seen in the special effects. While the effects on the '60s television series are pretty good, they were used just to communicate information, such as showing the

Enterprise orbiting a planet, traveling in space, etc. But by the time STAR TREK—THE MOTION PICTURE was made, special effects had become a motion picture star in their own right. What STAR WARS had done in such a spectacular fashion, other science fiction films were expected to equal or outdo. For a time this resulted in the kind of awesome visuals seen in some sequences of ST—TMP which seem to be there for no other reason than to wow the audience.

Even in STAR TREK—THE NEXT GENERATION some of the early episodes indulged in this to some degree, particularly in the premiere, "Encounter At Farpoint," and in "Where No One Has Gone Before." The main problem with the overemphasis on special effects is that they are sometimes regarded as something which can save a story when the script has failed to generation the atmosphere and sense of wonder which is required. Some clever matte paintings can be found in such original episodes as "The Menagerie," "Where No Man Has Gone Before," "Court Martial" and "Devil In The Dark," but they appear on screen for only a few seconds and don't linger long enough for the audience to stare at them in rapt fascination.

HEART AND SOUL

STAR TREK was about the people first. The show was script driven, not technology driven. Had it been otherwise it would have quickly turned into something lumbering and mind-numbing like BATTLESTAR: GALACTICA. In spite of network opposition, Gene Roddenberry and his talented staff turned out a carefully crafted series which succeeded more often than it failed, and told stories which often still stand up to scrutiny 25 years later.

On a week to week basis there may be more craft evident in an average episode of NEXT GENERATION when compared to an average episode of Trek Classic, but TNG has yet to hit as many highs in the script department as the original STAR TREK did. As good as TNG is, it hasn't produced very many episodes as good as "This Side of Paradise," "The Menagerie" and "City On The Edge of Forever" which will still be fascinating to watch 25 years from now.

Technically TNG is better produced than the old STAR TREK series was, but the writing is particularly lacking in the dialogue department. It's uncommon to find a Trek Classic episode in which a form of slang common to the '60s is used, but THE NEXT GENERATION often employs cliché's common to speech in the '80s and '90s, which will sound especially corny and annoying twenty years from now.

While women in Trek Classic tend to wear skimpy garments cut to within an inch of what network censors would tolerate, female characters are not really treated much better on the modern versions of STAR TREK. Gates MacFadden and Marina Sirtis have both mentioned how weak their roles are. Gates even remarked that if they were written the way women will doubtlessly be in the 24th century, as the exact emotional equals of men, Paramount is afraid that a sizable part of the audience would tune out. The studio apparently feels that people want to be assured that males will always be the dominant sex in our culture.

A SHOW WITH SOMETHING TO SAY

STAR TREK in the sixties still managed to inspire people with what it had to say and what it showed us. By suggesting that such a glittering future was not only probable but possible, it inspired people to want to be a part of that future. There are scientists today working for NASA, the military and elsewhere who were inspired as children to see the exciting possibilities in science and the ways it could affect the future. STAR TREK is still infecting people with that excitement today.

The diagnostic beds shown in the sickbay in Trek Classic are gradually becoming a reality—hundreds of years early. This is because people saw them portrayed on STAR TREK and realized what a good idea they were. Computers can talk now almost as well as the unnamed computers on Trek Classic could, and the computer voice technology is improving every day— hundreds of years before the era of STAR TREK. Would the people working in these areas of technology have thought to pursue them if they hadn't seen the possibilities suggested by STAR TREK? While STAR TREK hasn't created any sort of technological revolution, it has contributed to the notion that technol-

LEONARD NIMOY

ogy is not bad in and of itself. By the mid-sixties this was a pretty solid notion thanks to the proliferation of nuclear weapons.

AT THE CLIMAX OF THE SIXTIES

What STAR TREK could not do, perhaps because it had left the air by then, was help maintain a healthy popular interest in space exploration. By 1970, many people were questioning the value of space travel. How could it benefit us here on Earth? Unfortunately NASA was not up to the task of answering that question, nor have they managed to pull together a publicity campaign which has proven itself equal to the task to this day. Perhaps they should have hired some of the people behind STAR TREK to show them how to touch people with a bit of future lore, because that lore created in the sixties is still touching people with its limitless possibilities today.

STAR TREK ended with the sixties as though it were a product of the time rather than a reflection of a growing interest in the future. It was that interest in things to come which would keep the spirit of STAR TREK alive and eventually result in a sequel to Roddenberry's science fiction dream.

CHAPTER 2

ANOTHER SIDE OF STAR TREK

When Gene Roddenberry created THE NEXT GENERATION as a spin-off from STAR TREK, he largely just made superficial changes. But in keeping many basic elements intact, he not only continued using the good, but the problematical as well, while also creating a whole new arena filled with booby traps.

When Paramount announced that Gene Roddenberry was creating the first STAR TREK spin-off series, and that it would be set 75 years beyond the Trek universe we were all familiar with, it was inevitable that this meant changes. But how sweeping would those changes be? Clearly the technology would be updated, just as it had been for the motion pictures. But would the philosophy behind the show need to be retooled as well?

Since Gene Roddenberry understood his audience, he did not stray far from the tried and true when he recreated STAR TREK. Andrew Probert, who had contributed to the redesign of the Enterprise for STAR TREK: THE MOTION PICTURE, was tapped for the job of redesigning the Enterprise for its new, and far more advanced version. Although looking more sleek with a slightly squashed appearance, it still looked like the old Enterprise. The biggest change was the Holodeck. The kinds of recreation areas on the original Enterprise were rarely referred to outside of STAR TREK: THE MOTION PICTURE.

The other design alterations extended to the expected: the uniforms, hand weapons and other items such as the Tricorder. Just as they had been redesigned for the STAR TREK movies, they were redesigned for the TV series. Again, the designs were pretty superficial and seemed to have been done mostly for purposes of merchandising. More new STAR TREK toys could now be licensed by Paramount.

Although set 75 years after the original series, the changes were not that major the way technological changes would be after three-quarters of a century. By making the changes so slight, Roddenberry insured that the classic STAR TREK fans would more willingly accept this new version in spite of the completely new cast. In fact had the old cast been used along with all of the visual changes, viewers would have readily accepted it just as they had already accepted such cosmetic changes in the motion pictures.

FINE TUNING TREK PHILOSOPHY

Since Gene Roddenberry was closely involved in creating STAR TREK: THE NEXT GENERATION, it's not surprising that the underlying philosophy remained pretty much the same. If anything Roddenberry just expanded and deepened it. Whereas he had originally created the Klingons as superficial black-hat villains, he came to regret that short-sighted approach and went in completely the opposite direction in THE NEXT GENERATION. Instead of villains, the Klingons became a proud and honorable, if brutal, race. Although one could argue about how honorable they were with all the back-stabbing demonstrated in such episodes as "Sins of the Father" and "Redemption."

So Gene Roddenberry did expand the Trek philosophy, and perhaps a little too far. Roddenberry decided that his crew of the Enterprise-D would, frankly, be perfect. He decreed that they would get along without complaint and never have the kind of personality clashes experienced by Kirk, Spock and McCoy. They are always in agreement. The only time disagreements appear is when someone who is not a part of this tightly knit inner circle comes aboard.

Otherwise the main crew members, consisting of Picard, Riker, Data, Dr. Crusher, Geordi and Troi are always in harmony. Worf is the only wild card but then he's allowed to be—he isn't human. Tasha Yar seemed to have the makings of a character with spunk and personality, but she was quickly dispensed with.

Roddenberry remained the eternal optimist, in spite of all of the failures, disappointments and difficult times he had endured during the years between the cancellation of STAR TREK in 1969 and its return to life in 1979. Roddenberry continued to promote his philosophy of life which consisted of bold optimism (there will be a future and it will be wonderful), a belief in social progress, the benefits of technological advancement, the pursuit of knowledge, life affirmation, the tolerance of other cultures and Secular Humanism.

MAKING THE OLD WAYS BETTER

It is because Roddenberry's basic STAR TREK philosophy had been reinterpreted and sometimes altered in the motion picture treatments that he made certain that all of his beliefs for the STAR TREK universe were firmly in place and nailed down for THE NEXT GENERATION. With an underlying philosophy the shows therefore exhibit a point of view and occasionally moralize. But that's STAR TREK all over.

There were occasional contradictions in that philosophy which Roddenberry himself sought to correct in THE NEXT GENERATION. Instead of having the Klingons dismissed as being just the bad guys, he rewrote them as a proud warrior race with a culture as deep and diverse as anything seen on the other worlds in the Federation.

THE NEXT GENERATION continues the use of the Transporter with little alteration other than in the visual effects and the sound. This is explained by the difference in technology as in "Relics" when a ship is found with the old style Transporter. The old style sound effect is used when the Transporter beam materializes. But the Transporter is perhaps the prime example of STAR TREK magic. Created for the convenience of scriptwriters, it allows for the characters to move from the ship to a planet, and back again instantaneously, thereby dispensing with scenes of ships landing and taking off again. But the concept behind the Transporter is essentially science fiction magic which has always dodged any sort of logical explanation.

MAGIC OF MATTER TRANSMISSION

The concept of matter transmission aside, even if one accepts it, the Transporter would need more than just a beam out device, but also a beam in device as well. Otherwise what one has is something along the lines of a radio beam with no receiver, and yet the beam is "heard" at the other end. The beam materializes its cargo, whether human or otherwise, without the benefit of a receiver. The apparatus aboard the Enterprise does the job of being both sender and receiver and controls the contact at the other end of the beam. No explanation of how this is accomplished has ever been forthcoming. It's akin to projecting a flashlight beam which controls how far it throws the light precisely to the millimeter and not a fraction of a meter farther. The fact that it has been a part of STAR TREK lore since 1966 has made it accepted. It's akin to what in legalese is called "a grandfather clause"—it has been in effect so long that its length of existence justifies its continued existence. Only rarely are people shown being Transported from one Transporter unit to another.

Based only on what we have seen, the Transporter as it has been used in Trek Classic, the animated STAR TREK and THE NEXT GENERATION, has the capability of unlocking the secrets of immortality. Due to the storing of a person's pattern from earlier uses of the beam, this pattern could be applied some years later to restore one's youth, as it was in "Unnatural Selection" in the second year of THE NEXT GENERATION. That one episode suggests that the Transporter is a miracle device with multiple uses. Without exaggeration it could literally be described as an immortality instrument.

REWRITING THE RULES OF REALITY

~Which brings us to another device of magical technology: the holodeck. The holodeck which Roddenberry introduced on THE NEXT GENERATION clearly alters our views of what is possible in reality in any number of ways. The computer can be programmed to create virtually anything in the holodeck, from the lush surface of a planet with jungles and a waterfall to London in the 1890's. And unlike holograms which are intangible, the holodeck creates images of substance. In "The Big Goodbye" those images strike back with potentially deadly force. In that Peabody Award winning episode, Captain Picard creates a realm in the holodeck based on his favorite detective stories. Set in the 1930's, Dixon Hill is clearly based on the hard boiled detective thrillers of Raymond Chandler and Dashiell Hammett. Like Sherlock Holmes (another detective series), they are archetypes which are very much a part of their era—Holmes in London of the late 19th century and Dixon Hill in America of the early 20th century.

It's not unusual that a science fiction series should be so captivated by images from detective stories. Mystery fiction tends to be very popular among screenwriters and science fiction writers. Using this to create a film noir setting, THE NEXT GENERATION created a tech noire in which the holodeck world became a reality unto itself. The people created by the computer evidently are not just images which move according to a design but have a sense of self which as time went on was enhanced, as shown in "Elementary Dear Data." In "The Big Goodbye," the hologram people actually debated whether or not they were real and struggled to prove their individual reality. One of them, who possessed memories of a wife and family, even questioned what would happen to all of them when the program was ended? This question would ultimately be addressed in the sixth season episode "Moriarty."

A NEW SHIP AND NEW DREAMS

For his new STAR TREK series, Gene Roddenberry worked hard to produce a show that was true to the ideals of the first STAR TREK, but one which would nonetheless have its own flavor. As might be imagined, it took some doing; some of the characters took their time to settle in, but once they did, they were quite believable.

For starters, there was Captain Jean-Luc Picard. He was not to be the impetuous, dashing hothead Kirk had been, but rather an older, seasoned commander, well trained in the nuances of diplomatic relations, and with a long and distinguished career already behind him.

His new command, the Enterprise NCC 1701-D, was the first of a new class of vessels; its complement of over a thousand included entire families, as the lengthy space voyages it undertakes would otherwise keep families apart for years. It is, in essence, a world unto itself.

Filling out Picard's inner circle are a disparate group of characters.

Commander William Riker. Reminiscent of a young Captain Kirk, Riker is nonetheless an individual in his own right and one who goes boldly where starship captains are not allowed in the 24th century. Riker normally leads the Away Teams (the new name given to landing parties), which Starfleet has forbidden starship captains to head up if there is the slightest element of danger involved.

THE CAST OF STAR TREK: THE NEXT GENERATION.

JONATHAN FRAKES AND PATRICK STEWART AT PARAMOUNT'S 25TH ANNIVERSARY OF STAR TREK BASH..

© 1991
Ortega/Galella
Ltd.

Originally dubbed a Spock clone, the android Data has grown into a unique character in his own right. The only android serving in Starfleet, he is accepted by his comrades and has proven to be a vital member of the bridge crew on many occasions. His distinguished accomplishments have granted him the position of authority on the Enterprise of second officer, right behind Commander Riker. Data has spent many years trying to understand human beings in the hope that it will enable him to better understand himself.

Geordi LaForge began his stint on the Enterprise as a helmsman but was soon transferred to Engineering where his true talents have emerged. He knows more about the technological capabilities of the Enterprise than any other person aboard and is continually called upon to prove himself as well as prove what the flagship of Starfleet is capable of.

Something new in the 24th century is the ship's counselor. Part of the medical team, the counselor deals with the psychological health of the crew, and Deanna Troi has proven herself to be an extraordinary choice for this position.

Beverly Crusher is the ship's chief surgeon. Although she took a one year leave of absence early in the mission of the Enterprise-D, she soon returned and has participated in experiments and discoveries which are considered breakthroughs even in the 24th century. Beverly lived on the Enterprise with her son, Wesley, until he became old enough to join Starfleet.

Tasha Yar was a regular only on the first season, and the poor scripts on the series, as well as a distinct lack of understanding by the writers on what to do with her character, finally caused Denise Crosby to leave the series. Although killed off in "Skin of Evil," she returned in season three's stunning "Yesterday's Enterprise" for a more proper send-off.

WHAT WOULD KIRK HAVE THOUGHT?

The most controversial member of the Enterprise crew is Worf, a Klingon. Orphaned as a child at the battle of Khitomer, Worf was raised by humans on Earth. They did not deny the Klingon boy access to his heritage, though, so Worf has grown into a proud Klingon warrior who fully embraces his heritage and ancestry. Because he didn't grow up among other

Klingons, he is sometimes treated with suspicion by members of his own race, but Worf has managed to overcome this and has faced the Klingon high council itself on more than one occasion.

In the 24th century, the Klingon Armistice has held for more than 70 years and the Klingons have remained an important ally of the Federation. As a member in good standing of the Enterprise crew, Worf has advanced rapidly in rank until now he is the ship's security officer, a concept which would not have given James Kirk much security 75 years before.

But unlike the Klingons of a bygone time who despised all other races, Worf admires his human colleagues and has even become a more than fair poker player in his weekly games with Riker, Data and Dr. Crusher. With Data and Worf at the same table, it's hard to tell who is better at bluffing.

SIX YEARS ABOARD THE ENTERPRISE

Although Roddenberry was intensely involved with the creation and development of STAR TREK—THE NEXT GENERATION, the show had problems from the start.

In spite of a series bible which established who all of the regular characters were, no detailed background had been worked out for those characters. Their personalities were largely being established along the way by the actors and their various directors, with a result that the characters were often inconsistent from one episode to the next, particularly Captain Picard.

Worf was a late entry in the character roster because initially Roddenberry didn't want to bring the Klingons back. He thought they were simplistic villains and STAR TREK III—THE SEARCH FOR SPOCK had just emphasized the shortcomings of those characters even more. It was only when he decided to give the Klingons a real background and make them richer characters that he agreed to bring them back. But the series bible which the writers had been working on for the first season of TNG did not include Worf. That's how late his addition to the Enterprise family came.

AIMING FOR THE STARS

In spite of the fact that episode twelve of NEXT GENERATION, "The Big Goodbye," won the coveted Peabody Award for television excellence, far too many of the first year episodes of NEXT GENERATION suffered from a distinct lack of excellence. One of the other few exceptions is "Heart of Glory," the episode which established Worf as being more than just a fixture on the bridge.

The second year of NEXT GENERATION improved consistently, demonstrating that all involved had learned from their mistakes (and the mistakes of others) and were ready to finally get down to work.

Seasons three through six have continued the process of fine tuning the characters and establishing them as larger than life individuals in their own right. Picard has gone from being an inconsistent leader to a seasoned starship captain worthy of the position as commander of the flagship of Starfleet. Episodes have been done which have spotlighted both the many facets of Jean-Luc Picard while capitalizing on the fine acting abilities of actor Patrick Stewart.

Riker was the steadiest of the crew from the beginning, and subsequent seasons have only insured that he became even more firmly established as the finest first officer in Starfleet.

Data, who has no emotions, has been at the center of some of the most moving stories told in the series, including "Pen Pals" and "Hero Worship."

By year four even the female characters, Deanna Troi and Dr. Crusher, were getting episodes which spotlighted them in powerful stories such as "Remember Me" and "Power Play."

LOOKING FORWARD

While all too many series have run out of steam long before they complete six seasons, and start repeating themselves endlessly, NEXT GENERATION has continued to search for ways to grow and strengthen itself. The series carries with it a proud legacy. It is not just a STAR TREK spin-off, but it was shepherded by the Great Bird of the Galaxy himself, Gene Roddenberry. The dream Roddenberry first brought to life in 1966 has been revised and expanded while Gene looked on like the proud parent that he was.

The dream called STAR TREK has lasted for more than 27 years, and with THE NEXT GENERATION giving it new life and exploring new directions established by the original crew, it's evident that Roddenberry's dream will never die.

CHAPTER 3

THE CREW: FACE TO FACE

While THE NEXT GENERATION started with a clean slate and a new crew, how different were they from the familiar faces on the Enterprise?

The 23rd century will see the first starship named Enterprise. The 24th century will see the fourth, or so television history tells it. But it tells us other things as well. It tells about a valiant crew led by James Kirk and Commander Spock, and both are supported with undying loyalty by Dr. McCoy, Montgomery Scott, Lt. Uhura, Lt. Sulu and Ensign Chekov. Professionals all and all have something of value to contribute to the ongoing missions of the 23rd century Enterprise.

In the 24th century the Enterprise-D has been on the go for six years, and in command is Captain Jean-Luc Picard, the seasoned leader. Joining him on the Enterprise for the first time is a crew who would come to regard each other as friends just as much as the old Enterprise crew did seventy-five years before. Following Picard are Lt. William Riker, Commander Data, Geordi LaForge, Deanna Troi, Beverly Crusher and for a brief time there was Ensign Ro. One could also throw Guinan into that mix, but that centuries old confidant has no counterpart in the history of the Enterprise. She just listens, observes and on occasion offers sage advice. Although she lived well before the original Enterprise was launched, there is no record of her ever having crossed paths with Kirk and company.

Seventy-five years separates these two crews and their on-going missions aboard the Enterprise. How much has time

PATRICK
STEWART
AND
WILLIAM
SHATNER
— THE
TWO CAP-
TAINS OF
THE ENTER-
PRISE
MEET!

NICHELLE
NICHOLS
AND
WHOOPI
GOLDBERG.

© 1991
Ortega/Galell
a Ltd.

changed the Enterprise and its crew? Or how little has it changed it?

IN THE CENTER SEAT

James T. Kirk and Jean-Luc Picard. Both are commanders of the Enterprise at different points of future history and their styles of command are just as different as the kinds of starships they occupy.

The Enterprise of the time of James Kirk is an exploratory vessel, the flagship of the Federation and also its prime mover in certain instances of political persuasion. While the Federation is an alliance of many disparate worlds, the starships which represent it are outfitted with a crew who bear military ranks and who respond to situations accordingly. While the Prime Directive is supposed to prevent interference with emerging worlds which are not yet a part of the Federation, Kirk has often been required to respond to situations militarily.

Although likable and humane, Kirk is a stern commander who takes his responsibilities seriously. To him the Enterprise is the most important thing in his life, but he bears the burden of command well. He loves it. He has a passion for command and a zest for the life of a space explorer. To Kirk, facing the unknown is what gives life its meaning.

Prior to Kirk was Christopher Pike, an Enterprise commander who, although liked and respected by those under his command, did not bear the continuing demands of command so easily. Following an encounter on Rigel VII in which he recognized too late the threats posed by a warrior tribe, Pike considered resigning his commission and becoming an Orion trader. At least then people wouldn't die if he made a mistake. Although he finally remained with the Federation, he was a grimly determined leader who finally accepted a promotion off the Enterprise and away from the life of a starship captain.

SURRENDER?—NEVER!

Many fans of Trek Classic were bothered by the actions of Jean-Luc Picard in "Encounter At Farpoint" for one very specific reason—he surrendered the Enterprise. Up to that point, in all of the adventures of the original STAR TREK crew then presented, Captain Kirk had never surrendered the Enterprise. In fact in STAR TREK III—THE VOYAGE HOME, even when surrender seemed the only alternative, Kirk destroyed the Enterprise rather than see it fall into enemy hands. As Kirk stood on the Genesis planet, watching the Enterprise fall through the atmosphere in a blaze of meteoric glory, he questioned the wisdom of that decision. But his crew supported him, stating that it was the only thing he could have done.

When Jean-Luc Picard surrendered the Enterprise on the very first voyage we were witness to, many viewers were shocked. The captain of the Enterprise surrendering? Unheard of! It was so unheard of that when Captain Kirk finally uttered the words "I surrender" in STAR TREK VI—THE UNDISCOV-ERED COUNTRY, it was intended to come as a surprise because in 25 years he'd never uttered that phrase in his position as commander of the Enterprise.

Even when the Enterprise was imprisoned by V'ger in STAR TREK—THE MOTION PICTURE, Kirk began the self destruct sequence rather than allow V'ger to carry out its threats against the Earth while the Enterprise sat helplessly by. Kirk countermanded that order minutes later when he saw that it was unnecessary, but even then he was willing to sacrifice his vessel rather than surrender in the face of seemingly hopeless odds. To Kirk a fight was never hopeless. There was always alternative. As he said in THE WRATH OF KHAN. "I've tricked death. I've cheated death. But I've never had to face death."

The problem with Jean-Luc Picard is not in himself so much as it is within his vessel. The Enterprise-D is not Jim Kirk's Enterprise. There were no families and children on the first starship Enterprise, nor would Kirk have tolerated such a thing. To Kirk this would have been a reckless experiment of the highest order, no matter how high minded the ideals behind it.

THE IDEAL ENTERPRISE

While Gene Roddenberry long maintained that the Enterprise was not a warship, it certainly acted like one! The military ranks aside, the Enterprise was well armed and those aboard were clearly battle-trained. Captain Kirk was a man well versed in the strategy of war. While the Klingons of Picard's day have joined arm in arm with the Federation, Kirk had no such luxury. To Kirk, an encounter with a Klingon vessel marked a skirmish in a cold war, just as an encounter with a Romulan ship inevitably did when it took place outside the Neutral Zone.

75 years later, Jean-Luc Picard commands an Enterprise in a realm where the Klingons are part of the Federation, just as the Organians had predicted to James Kirk many years before in the encounter referred to in the Trek Classic annals as "Errand Of Mercy." That prediction of peace had won out and the Enterprise under Jean-Luc Picard could truly be called a ship of peace. After all, warships don't carry the families and children of the personnel assigned to the vessel any more than 20th century military vessels did. In this way the Enterprise of James T. Kirk had its origins in the 20th century much more than Jean-Luc Picard's Enterprise does.

But does this mitigate Picard's decision to surrender? In the face of the seemingly merciless cruelty of Q, could Picard have really believed that the Enterprise would have been any more safe than if he had faced that omnipotent being's wrath? In "Encounter At Farpoint" the Enterprise had performed a saucer-separation in the hope of separating the families from the dangers of conflict, but it had proven to be a futile act.

It may well have been the clear and present danger to non-combat personnel that fueled Picard's expressed resentment towards having children on the Enterprise. Their presence tied his hands because however innocent the rest of the crew may have been in the face of outside threats, they had accepted these risks when they signed on. But what about adolescent and pre-adolescent children? Clearly they were incapable of such an informed consent when they came aboard the Enterprise-D.

These then are the hard questions Picard has to face when the Enterprise is placed in imminent danger. While Captain Kirk was clearly not one to surrender, neither did he have to face the added burden of having children who would suffer the consequences of his actions. So when Picard is criticized for surrendering in the face of adversity, his ship bearing a personnel roster of one thousand is not just larger than Kirk's ship of four hundred, but bears added ethical considerations as well.

PARALLELS AND DIFFERENCES

So the vessels commanded by James Kirk and Jean-Luc Picard are not the same Enterprise, either visually or philosophically. It is because of this that different styles of command are quite clearly forced on the two men. Might they have been similar in their command of the center seat had history not changed so much during the intervening three-quarters of a century? Even so, there are some similarities between the two starship captains.

Kirk was born on a farm in Iowa and Picard grew up on a vineyard in France. Similarly, both had their eyes on a future which had nothing to do with keeping both feet on the ground. Picard and Kirk both have older brothers with whom they often disagreed and parted on bad terms. In Kirk's case he ultimately saw his brother, George, die as a result of an attack on a Federation colony in the incident called "Operation: Annihilate." Picard, on the other hand, made up with his brother and each came to terms with the divergent paths their lives had taken.

Both Kirk and Picard have an undying love of adventure. In Picard's case this initially revealed itself in an intense interest in interplanetary archeology. Picard was such a gifted student that his teacher, Prof. Galen, believed that Jean-Luc could have been the finest archaeologist of his generation. But as fulfilling as Picard found the explorations into the glittering history of alien worlds, he was drawn even more strongly to the endless possibilities of history yet to come. The Federation was making that history and in Starfleet Jean-Luc could be a part of it.

ADVENTURE!

To seek out new life and new civilizations. These are the dreams of both James Kirk and Jean-Luc Picard, and both chose to do this with a quick mind and a willingness to try to understand the new discoveries and new civilizations and their impact on the Federation.

The Starfleet Academy experiences of Kirk and Picard were different and this led them in different directions.

As a student, Kirk was grimly determined to succeed. While he made friends such as Gary Mitchell, he also made enemies, such as Finnegan. Kirk attempted to keep out of the upper classman's way, but the bully took joy in making Jim Kirk's life miserable.

Kirk refused to be baited and let Finnegan dig his own grave until the upper classman was expelled in a cheating scandal.

This moral triumph wasn't enough for Kirk. Deep down he wished for a more fitting climax to their conflict, and years later, in the "Shore Leave" incident, Kirk found himself confronted by a duplicate of Finnegan whom he proceeded to beat up. The fact that Finnegan gave as good as he got made the final battle all the more perfect.

Picard was not so grim a student as Kirk, and in fact allowed himself to become drawn into a brawl. As a result, Picard was stabbed in the back and would have died had not immediate medical attention and an artificial heart saved his life. This made Picard realize how precious and fragile life is. As a result he worked hard after his graduation from Starfleet to achieve his goals. Picard and Kirk were both young when they were posted to their first commands.

THE NEW CAPTAIN

When Kirk became Captain of the Enterprise, he was following in the footsteps of Christopher Pike, a much admired officer in Starfleet. In fact Kirk largely inherited Pike's hand-picked crew and knew that he would have a lot to live up to. This is when Kirk first met Mr. Spock, his Vulcan Science Officer. Starfleet ordered Kirk to retain the Vulcan in the post Spock had earned even though Captain Kirk had wanted to make Gary Mitchell his first officer. But Mitchell lacked the experience, and as it turned out Kirk would come to realize that Spock was indeed the best man for the job.

Picard was also young when posted to his first command, although unlike Kirk, it was not to the Enterprise. Picard's first command was the science vessel Stargazer, whose mission was not unlike that initial one Kirk had for the Enterprise. But while Kirk embarked on a five year mission and then returned to Earth, Picard took the Stargazer on a deep space mission which lasted for twenty-two years. As commander of the Stargazer, Picard was also able to put his expertise in exo archaeology to good use.

When Picard returned from his mission he was considered a hero, even though the Stargazer had been lost in a battle with a mysterious alien vessel. It would be years before Picard learned that the aliens were the Ferengi, and that he had made the first Federation contact with them, albeit in combat. But it was this mission which would lead to Picard being given command of the recently christened Enterprise-D, the flagship of the Federation.

DEATH IN DEEP SPACE

Kirk was much younger than Picard when he experienced his first death of a crewman under his command. In Kirk's case it was his old friend, Gary Mitchell. What happened to Mitchell was no more his fault than it was Kirk's, but a cruel fate had brought them together and forced Kirk to make the inescapable decision that resulted in Mitchell's death. Kirk had known Gary since their days together in Starfleet Academy, and the tragedy personalized death for him in a way he had not expected.

Kirk had been just a crewman when he saw several of his landing party team die from an attack by a vampire cloud. Years later Kirk encountered this entity again and faced the responsibility he felt for those earlier deaths, which he had blamed on himself for not acting swiftly enough years before. He finally came to realize that there was nothing he could have done at the time to change what happened.

Picard was not so directly involved in the death of his good friend Jack Crusher, but the burden he felt was just as great. Picard had assigned Crusher to the Away Team which met disaster, and he accompanied his friend's body back to Earth. As Captain of the Stargazer, Picard felt honor bound to meet with Crusher's widow, Beverly, and Jack's young son, Wesley. The incident made Picard all the more painfully aware of the aftermath of a crew person's death. When he found that the Enterprise-D would contain whole families, Picard could only recall the dangers and death he had encountered aboard the

Stargazer. Both men would encounter death many more times, including ways that would be painfully memorable.

Kirk discovered that he had a grown son, but within months of this discovery the young man was brutally slain by Klingons, which resulted in Kirk harboring a deep hatred for that alien race. Kirk finally overcame this grudge only with a supreme effort. When the Federation made peace with the Klingon Empire, so too did James Kirk.

One of the death's Picard found hardest to reconcile was the swift and senseless death of Tasha Yar. Killed on an Away Team mission, Yar had died long before her time, her life snuffed out by the brutal gesture of an alien entity. All deaths were hard on Picard, but this was another death of a close friend.

THE FIRST OFFICERS

Kirk and Picard have very different first officers, and yet in many respects their relationships with them are similar.

Kirk found himself coming to better understand his first officer, Spock, after the death of Gary Mitchell. Spock had uncharacteristically expressed feelings for what Mitchell had endured. This revealed much about the Vulcan to Kirk that he had not previously suspected was there. Although Spock's studied reserve was hard to penetrate, a mutual respect eventually became a life long friendship.

Picard's own first officer, William Riker, was clearly the best man for the job. Although they had not met before, Picard was well aware of Riker's abilities and knew that Commander Riker was ready for his own starship captaincy. In fact, he could have had it but requested the first officer station on the Enterprise-D, the Federation flagship.

While Kirk was quick to place himself at the head of a landing party, by the time of Picard's day the Federation had forbidden such reckless practices by a man as experienced as a starship captain. Picard chafed under the restrictions Riker was quick to remind him of. If there was any question of safety, Riker would lead the Away Team. This would place an experienced officer in charge to deal with the demands of the mission while not leaving the starship without its captain should something go wrong. Picard secretly believed that Riker enjoyed telling his captain that he couldn't do something.

THE KIRK SYNDROME

What Picard resented was a situation many believe was brought about by the actions of James T. Kirk all those years before. Kirk would unhesitatingly run in where angels feared to tread, and he often took his highly experienced first officer, Spock, with him. Had anything happened to them, the Enterprise had no one else aboard with even half the training and experience of either Kirk or Spock.

Spock had been aboard the Enterprise for eleven years when Kirk took command. Kirk had been considered such an outstanding officer that he had been selected to succeed Christopher Pike on the flagship of Starfleet. But Kirk was not one to sit back and let someone else take any risks that he wasn't prepared to take himself. This included boarding a derelict spacecraft.

When Kirk encountered the crippled sister ship the Constellation adrift in space, he beamed over with the maintenance crew to supervise repairs personally. As a result, Commodore Decker, the sole survivor of the crew of the Constellation, recovered in sickbay aboard the Enterprise and then relieved Spock of command due to his being the senior officer aboard ship.

Decker placed the Enterprise in deadly danger until Kirk was able to forcibly relieve him of duty. Had Kirk remained aboard the Enterprise to begin with, the vessel never would have been endangered. That would not be the last time that Kirk's love of adventure threatened the well being of his beloved starship.

And love the Enterprise Kirk most certainly did. He considered the vessel a part of his life. In the incident called "The Naked Time," while other crew members were revealing their secret fears and desires, Kirk's secret was that he put the Enterprise first, before everything, even before his own inner needs. He would do anything to save the Enterprise; take any risk. It remained the one great love of his life.

MARRIED TO THE ENTERPRISE

When Kirk's five year mission ended he was promoted to Admiral and stationed back on Earth where he lectured and taught at Starfleet Academy. But in space, his only true love awaited his return.

While Kirk did not avoid relationships with women, they were inevitably brief and unhappy. Even his relationship with Carol Marcus, which produced a son, was hidden from him for more than twenty years. People tended to stay angry at Kirk a long time. His relationships with Edith Keeler, Rayna and with Miramanee were even more unhappy as all those women died! It was perhaps inevitable that the Enterprise would be destroyed as well.

After a few years on Earth, Kirk felt restless and knew he had to get the Enterprise back. When the Earth was threatened by a menace which only the Enterprise was available to face, Kirk used his clout and years of deep space experience to regain command, and one way or another he retained that command for years to come. No woman could ever be as powerful an influence on his heart as the Enterprise was.

But as seriously as Picard takes his role of Captain of the Enterprise, he does not appear to be as powerfully attached to the ship as Kirk is. The fact that Picard surrendered the Enterprise in "Encounter At Farpoint" seems to indicate that. I keep coming back to that only because it is a pivotal incident which is the opposite of what Jim Kirk, time and again, demonstrated under similar circumstances.

If Picard is married to anything it is to his career, not to a specific vessel. As much as the Enterprise means to him he clearly expressed equal admiration for his first command, the Stargazer, when that vessel was found intact in the incident described as "The Battle." There Picard demonstrated his own command of modern battle tactics which clearly make him the equal of Kirk in many situations.

WHAT TO DO?

A common criticism of Picard during his early days of command aboard the Enterprise was a seeming indecisiveness. When put in a critical situation, Picard would gather his bridge crew and ask for suggestions before moving forward. Kirk, on the other hand, would only ask for specific input of information from his bridge officers, not for their opinions. Kirk would make a decision and stick to it, not worrying what someone else said or thought. Dr. McCoy was often willing to question Kirk's decisions, a fact Kirk sometimes resented. That Kirk's judgment generally was proven to be sound didn't stop McCoy from questioning on other occasions.

Picard often called on Riker for input regarding important decisions, and a couple years later would turn to Guinan as well. The most stunning example of this is in "Yesterday's Enterprise" when Guinan tells Picard that, incredible as it might seem, the timeline had altered and Tasha Yar shouldn't still exist! Picard has such faith in Guinan that he accepts what she tells him even though there is no way for her to prove anything to him.

Although Picard initially resists, he finally accepts what she has to say as fact. Even if Spock had come to Kirk with a story like that, it is questionable whether Kirk would have accepted it quite so readily. But then, in an altered timeline, was this really the same Picard? History changes personalities and the entire background of Picard in the altered timeline could be different, thereby making him a different person altogether.

In recent years, Picard has been more willing to make decisions without calling a meeting, and as a result he seems like a stronger commander. A man with all the experience Picard has, which is about as much experience as Kirk had by the time of the Klingon armistice, would not be unwilling to make a tough decision and stick with it.

THE PRIME DIRECTIVE

The Prime Directive prohibits Federation representatives from interfering in the normal development of a planetary society. Even though the Prime Directive existed in the time of James T. Kirk, Captain Kirk seemed to honor that directive more in the breach than in upholding it. Kirk tended to regard the Prime Directive as a suggestion which was left up to his discretion. If Captain Kirk encountered a planet whose society he didn't like, he set out to change it. In "Return of the Archons," when he finds a society ruled by a computer programmed by a long dead scientist, Kirk talks the machine into self-destructing. That society is thereby forever changed.

In "A Taste of Armageddon," when two planets which have been fighting a war via computer (rather than with bombs) for 500 years threatens Kirk and his crew, rather than merely escape, Kirk destroys the computers, forcing the two worlds to come to the bargaining table. It could be argued that this is a good thing, but it's clearly a violation of the Prime Directive. Many more examples exist.

Picard is more of a strict constructionist when it comes to upholding the Prime Directive. In fact in at least one episode, "Ensign Ro," the Federation is accused of hiding behind the Prime Directive. By not "getting involved" in civil wars, the Federation can claim the moral high ground by pointing to the Prime Directive. But not getting involved presumes there is no right or wrong in a dispute. For instance, in "Symbiosis" Picard encounters two worlds in which one has enslaved the other by addicting the populace to a drug.

Picard refuses to reveal the truth to the victims because of the non-interference clause of the Prime Directive. But using the same logic, he also refuses to help the exploiters repair their aging technology. Picard presumes that both sides will have to find alternative solutions to their problems, but he doesn't stay around to see whether or not this actually transpires.

NON-INTERFERENCE?

Like any political organization, the Federation apparently prefers not to get involved if it doesn't have to. But like any organization, its members don't always follow the party line. Kirk chose to use his own judgment based on the circumstances. In "Errand of Mercy," when the Federation and the Klingons clash over the non-aligned, primitive planet of Organia, Kirk tries to tell the Organians what they should do.

They refuse and don't want to get involved in any disputes between the Federation and the Klingon Empire. When Kirk's clashes with the Klingons escalate and a galactic war is on the verge of breaking out, the Organians reveal their unsuspected powers and impose their own brand of the Prime Directive by preventing the Klingons and the Federation from waging war. This not only shows the wisdom behind the Prime Directive, but also the fact that as honorable an idea as it may be, it falls apart if two equally matched powers are involved where only one side wants to uphold it.

Even though Picard believes in upholding the Prime Directive, he is often put to the test. In "Justice," when the Enterprise visits a peaceful society, Wesley Crusher is condemned to death by the unseen entity which rules that world, all because the boy accidentally broke one of their laws. Apparently on that world, breaking any law results in the death penalty. Picard is forced to intervene to save Wesley and does so by challenging the entity's notion of what justice is and how it can best be served. Whereas Captain Kirk would probably have talked the entity, computer, or whatever it is into self-destructing, Picard challenged it to a duel of ethics—and won.

Whereas Kirk would probably have brought the might of the Enterprise to bear, the vessel was disabled as life support had shut down and the temperature aboard ship was dropping. Since Picard didn't have those weapons at his disposal, we can't say for certain that he wouldn't have used them as a first resort, just as Kirk might have done. But with that option unavailable to him, Picard took not just the high road, but apparently the only road that was open to him. Clearly, Picard knows how to talk his way out of a situation as well as Kirk does.

MEN OF ACTION

Oddly enough, as THE NEXT GENERATION progressed, Picard has become a lot more like Kirk than he started out to be. Initially Picard came across as an elder statesman, a man of conservative demeanor who did not become directly involved with the conflicts. Riker was the man of action who would beam down to a planet and get into trouble, or visit another ship and get into trouble. Picard has had this thrust upon him more and more in recent years.

In the fifth season of NEXT GENERATION, Picard is in a turbolift with three children when the Enterprise encounters serious problems. Picard, although injured, must climb out of the turbolift and lead the children to safety, actions which required a lot of physical exertion.

Kirk got into fights in many episodes of Trek Classic because the original series was pitched as being an action/adventure series and it had to live up to that. Kirk was the one who always had the two-fisted action scenes, including one in "Mirror, Mirror" where he has a fist fight with the Spock of a parallel universe. In "Shore Leave" Kirk's fist fight is in two different scenes with the same character and lasts what seems like several minutes.

Until recently I would have said that Picard was nothing like this. The cool commander of the Enterprise-D studied his facts, made informed decisions and called security in the case of personal, physical threats. Nothing would have led us to believe that he was a man of physical action the way Kirk clearly fancied himself.

Then "Starship Mine" in the sixth season of NEXT GENERATION changed all that. When the Enterprise is evacuated for a radiation sweep, Picard returns to his quarters to retrieve his saddle. Jean-Luc intends to go horseback riding on the planet below. But before he can leave the Enterprise, he encounters an unfamiliar crewman. Realizing that the man is an intruder, Picard tries to subdue him and knocks him out. When Jean-Luc discovers that there are still more intruders aboard, he gets into a running battle with them, fighting when cornered and using weapons both primitive (a crossbow) and modern. He also relies on his wits. It's Picard as Capt. Kirk, and it works.

COMMANDING LOYALTY

While Picard has the respect and the admiration of his crew, they haven't been put to the test the same way that Kirk has tested his crew under fire. When Kirk determines that he must return to the Genesis planet to save Spock, in defiance of Starfleet orders, his inner circle all volunteer to help him steal the Enterprise. In so doing they put their lives and their careers on the line. The one previous time anything like this was done was when Spock hijacked the Enterprise in order to help Captain Christopher Pike, his former commander. Spock did this on his own without asking for help because he logically decided that no one else should be expected to face the consequences for what he was doing.

In Picard's case, when Starfleet asks him to penetrate a secret Cardassian base, Worf and Beverly Crusher agree to accompany him. Riker is ordered to remain on the Enterprise where a new Captain takes over command temporarily. The way Picard works well with people was never better exemplified than in "Chain of Command" when Riker and the new Captain of the Enterprise experience a vicious personality clash. In fact Riker comes close to being kicked off the ship due to his challenges of the new captain's authority. The other bridge crew don't get along with the new captain much better.

Picard's ease in getting along with his subordinates has long been taken for granted. While there were some initial signs of strain in the first season, this was smoothed over by season's end. Any residual resentment Beverly may have had towards Jean-Luc over the death of her husband, Jack Crusher, has long since evaporated. So it's interesting that while Classic Trek demonstrated the loyalty of Kirk's crew with direct action, THE NEXT GENERATION demonstrated it by indirect action. Absence makes the heart grow fonder, and in Picard's absence the carefully crafted Enterprise ensemble of his inner circle began to unravel.

FRIENDSHIPS

Kirk had only a couple close friends on the Enterprise; Spock and McCoy. Picard also has close friends, but he doesn't associate with them the same way they associate with their other friends. Picard and Riker associate, and Picard and Guinan do as well. But Picard is never a part of the poker games Riker has with Worf, Data and Beverly. The circles of friends overlap, but only slightly.

When Kirk went on shore leave, it tended to be with Spock and McCoy. Not with anyone else.

When Picard goes on shore leave it is to get away from the day to day demands of the Enterprise, and so he goes alone. Unlike Kirk, Picard seems more at ease with himself when he's alone. While he can be gregarious and friendly, fitting into a group of newcomers easily, he can be just as happy in the company of a soothing silence. The only time Picard seems to indulge in the recreational activities of his fellow crew members is when a play is being put on. Otherwise he doesn't mix with the crew very much during off duty hours.

Picard likes to read. The mystery stories featuring detective Dixon Hill are his favorites. Kirk likes to read as well. He loved the antique edition of A TALE OF TWO CITIES he received as a birthday present from Spock. Antique books are only appreciated by people who appreciate books as a whole.

ROMANCES

Kirk's romances have tended to be tinged with tragedy. Even the woman named Ruth, the simulacrum conjured up on the "Shore Leave" planet, is one he gets along with well primarily because she isn't real—just an android recreation of a girl he once knew.

Picard has had occasional romances which have flared briefly then gone their separate ways, just as many romances do in real life. Jean-Luc was briefly involved with a woman named Vash during a shore leave encounter, but as attractive as he found her, they were too unalike for it to last. She could never be a captain's wife.

Picard has met old flames, such as in "We'll Always Have Paris," and even became involved with one of his subordinates. But when she resented Picard displaying favoritism towards her by excusing her from dangerous assignments, a clash developed. When she went on an assignment and came close to death, both realized that their relationship wouldn't work while both of them were on the Enterprise.

Jean-Luc's attachment to his career (even more so than his ship) prevented him from resigning to be with the woman he loved. Starfleet is everything to Picard. Even when his old teacher, Prof. Galen, tried to lure Picard off the Enterprise with promises of galactic fame, Jean-Luc couldn't bring himself to walk away from his responsibilities.

Kirk and Picard live for adventure and for the discovery of what awaits them in the stars. As different as they are in some ways, they are very much alike in their need to experience the thrill of discovery. It is not surprising that each of them would wind up in the center seat on the Enterprise.

THE FIRST OFFICERS

They hold their positions on different starships with the same name, 75 years apart. Vulcan and human, could there really be anything in common between them other than the position of responsibility they hold on the starship, or are the differences between them more pronounced than the similarities?

In the days when Kirk was in command of the Enterprise, he usually led the landing parties, often with Spock at his side. It was Kirk's casual willingness to put himself in danger which eventually led to the alteration in the rules. If there is any possibility of danger, it is up to the first officer to advise the captain against being on the landing party, and it's the responsibility of the captain to follow that advice. The captain also has the option of deciding whether the first officer is correct and overriding his advisory. Even after Starfleet instituted this policy late in Kirk's Starfleet career, he often disagreed with his first officer's advisories and went ahead on the landing party anyway.

While commanding the Stargazer, Picard tended to override his then first officer's advisories, but Will Riker is not so easily dissuaded. Riker is a man with a dynamic personality who knows when he's right and stands up for those beliefs. When Riker believes that his captain could be putting himself in danger, he refuses to allow it to happen. Picard has reluctantly accepted this state of affairs because he knows that his first officer is right.

Another duty of the first officer is to relieve the captain in case of illness, or if he believes that the captain in unfit for command. This is an extreme situation which rarely arises.

Spock faced this situation twice. The first time was when Kirk took the Enterprise into the Romulan neutral zone and lied about the reasons. That time it turned out to be a subterfuge, but the second time was legitimate. When Spock determined that Kirk was being irrational in "Turnabout Intruder," he went to Dr. McCoy since the ship's doctor would have to support the first officer's decision.

Riker faced the same situation when Picard was replaced with a double. While the alien replacement meant no harm, looking like Picard is not the same as having the captain's judgment and experience.

SECOND IN COMMAND

Spock and Riker had each achieved distinction before they became linked to their most famous commanders. Spock served for eleven years under Captain Christopher Pike before James T. Kirk assumed command of the Enterprise. The Vulcan joined the command crew of the Enterprise shortly after graduating from Starfleet Academy.

Unlike Spock, Riker had to work his way up to the Enterprise. Prior to service aboard the Enterprise, Riker first served aboard the Potemkin, as a Lieutenant. With his concerns as single-mindedly on his career as Spock has been on his, Riker soon advanced to the rank of second officer with a transfer to the USS Yorktown. Distinguishing himself still further, he received a promotion to first officer on the USS Hood, which was commanded by Captain Jonathan DeSoto.

Riker has clearly been restless to move forward, remaining unsatisfied with his postings while doing his best to prove himself in those positions. Spock, who was posted to the Enterprise as his first assignment, was content to remain on that starship. Spock began as the science officer and while retaining that classification, worked his way up to first officer under Christopher Pike.

Riker had always been hell-bent to succeed. When he was informed that the Enterprise-D had been commissioned, he made it his goal to be that vessel's first officer, particularly when he learned that Jean-Luc Picard would be named Captain. Although Riker had reached the stage where he might have been posted to his own starship command, Will did not consider the transfer to the Enterprise from the Hood merely a lateral move. The Enterprise-D was the flagship of the Federation fleet and would be a far more prestigious and interesting position than the command of a lesser vessel would have been.

COMMAND POSITION

Riker has been offered the chance to command his own ship three times, but turned down each offer. Will is willing to wait for the Enterprise as no lesser vessel will suit him. But he is not in competition with Captain Picard. Riker doesn't consider his position as executive officer a secondary one by any means as he considers Picard to be the captain in Starfleet.

He prefers to serve under Picard until Jean-Luc opts for retirement rather than walk away from the most challenging and interesting opportunity he has ever faced. This may be a long wait as Jean-Luc has been offered a promotion to admiral and transfer three times, but has turned those options down as well. Picard is not yet ready to walk away from the life he has known for so long.

Spock has also turned down the chance to command his own starship, but for different reasons than Riker. Spock has certain ambitions, but they do not involve command. He likes being a science officer and prefers his science duties to the very different duties that would occupy his time should he accept a command of his own. In fact Spock eventually left Starfleet to follow in his father's footsteps and become a Vulcan ambassador.

To Spock, serving on the Enterprise was an opportunity to gain priceless experience meeting and exchanging information with new life forms and new civilizations. Such experience would serve him well in later years when, as an ambassador, he would be called upon to deal with alien cultures.

Riker did briefly achieve command of the Enterprise, but it was under circumstances he would have preferred not occur. When Picard was captured by the Borg and brainwashed by them, Riker had to not only take command of the Enterprise, but battle the Borg which were then under the leadership of Picard in his Borg form of Locutus. When Picard was rescued, Riker gladly returned the reins of command to his captain, and his friend.

DIVERGENT APPROACHES

Spock has taken a leave of absence from Starfleet more than once, such as after the Enterprise completed its first five year mission under the command of James T. Kirk. Spock went to explore his Vulcan roots, returning to the reconditioned Enterprise when the Federation faced a galactic threat. Spock remained with Kirk and the Enterprise thereafter. Not even a brief sojourn with death could keep him away from the Enterprise for very long.

Spock views Starfleet not for the opportunities for advancement that it offers someone as talented and ambitious as Will Riker, but for the opportunities to learn new things. There is no better place to learn than aboard a starship which is exploring the edge of the galactic frontier. In his later years Spock would push this still further when, as an ambassador, he would undertake a secret mission to Romulus to meet with a faction wishing to learn more about their Vulcan roots and possibly reunite the two cultures peacefully.

Although Spock and Riker are both able to inspire loyalty and respect in the crews they command, they achieve this in different ways. Spock's honesty, intellect and Vulcan charisma go far in impressing people. Starfleet personnel know that Spock not only makes intelligent choices, but that the choice is made after exhaustive analysis.

Riker's experience in Starfleet goes far in impressing his fellows, and he is also capable of great charm. But when Riker is displeased, he doesn't hide that displeasure for a second, and has engaged in personality clashes with fellow officers. Riker tends to clash with certain personality types while he gets along easily with others. But there seems to be no middle ground with him. Either he approves of someone or he doesn't.

DIVERGENT BACKGROUNDS

Spock and Riker couldn't be more different in their backgrounds. Spock was born on Vulcan to a human mother and a Vulcan father. Riker, on the other hand, was born on Earth in Alaska and is human through and through. While Spock engenders respect, the word "charming" couldn't precisely be used to describe him, even by those few he deems his friends.

Riker is affable and friendly and enjoys playing hard in his off hours and on shore leave. In the incident described as "The Game," a liaison that Riker had with a pleasure woman on a paradise planet led to his being manipulated into bringing a dangerous brainwashing device aboard the Enterprise. Riker chose his playmates more carefully thereafter.

As a Vulcan, Spock doesn't relax the way many other races do. Spock finds it relaxing to do math computations and read files in the computer's memory banks. Having an encyclopedic memory, he likes to add to his vast storehouse of knowledge. To Spock, learning is entertaining.

Spock long considered himself far removed from normal human concerns, believing that pure logic was the greatest thing a person could strive for. But events surrounding his encounter with V'ger, in which a vast machine intelligence which had achieved absolute logic required more to be truly alive, taught Spock a great deal about living. Following his own death and resurrection, Spock learned that recapturing what he was involved more than just replenishing his storehouse of knowledge. From his mother he once again learned that being able to feel something emotionally is not all bad, if practiced with Vulcan restraint.

FAMILY ESTRANGEMENT

In spite of growing up on worlds far apart both galactically and philosophically, some problems are common to all races. In the cases of Spock and Riker, neither got along well with their fathers.

Spock decided at a young age to follow the principles of the Vulcan way absolutely, but even this wasn't enough for his father. Sarek wanted Spock to remain on Vulcan after graduating from the Vulcan Science Academy and become an ambassador. But Spock felt he could accomplish more in Starfleet.

When Spock went behind his father's back and applied to Starfleet Academy, Sarek was as angry as a Vulcan can be without showing it. When Spock insisted on following his interests, which he believed Starfleet could best serve, Sarek cut off all communication with him and it was some fifteen years before they reconciled their estrangement.

In spite of the reconciliation during the "Journey To Babel" incident, Spock and Sarek had another falling out years

WIL WHEATON AND GATES MCFADDEN AT THE JUNE 6, 1991 25TH ANNIVERSARY OF STAR TREK BASH.

later, after Amanda had died and when Sarek had married his third wife, Perrin. Even though Sarek fell ill in his later years, he and his son never reconciled and Spock was away on a secret mission when Sarek finally died.

PARTIAL RECONCILIATION

Riker became estranged from his father, Kyle, when he was just a boy. Riker resented the way his father treated him after his mother died. Kyle Riker withdrew from his son after his wife died and Will resented it because that was the time he needed his father close to him more than ever. Although Will's father was in Starfleet, he didn't want his son to join. Will nonetheless applied himself vigorously in Starfleet and far outstripped his father's accomplishments.

Will Riker and his father also did not speak for fifteen years. In the incident known as "The Icarus Factor," Will was offered the command of the Ares, a ship which would soon be leaving on a deep space mission. In the twelve hours Will had to decide about accepting the promotion, a Starfleet officer was sent to brief him on the Ares mission. As luck would have it, that officer was Kyle Riker. Their initial meeting was strained but they finally worked out their differences, although Will still felt that his father had largely abandoned him as a child. Their reconciliation accomplished much, but Will remains far from feeling that he truly loves his father.

Interestingly, when Will Riker encountered his double in "Second Chances," they had their own differences to work out. When the second Riker decided to call himself Thomas, he dismissed the notion of reconciling with his father. Two Rikers. Two different choices. But then Will would have also dismissed the notion had he not been confronted with seeing his father again without any warning.

EXTRACURRICULAR ACTIVITIES

While Spock is not a shore leave kind of guy, he does have non-academic interests, such as playing the Vulcan lyre, a type of small harp.

Riker also plays a musical instrument, although it's not quite as genteel and ethereal; it's the trombone. But it works for him since Riker is more of a loud, brassy character compared to Spock's more quiet and reserved personality.

Riker is more like Kirk if he's like anyone, as he's a man of action in more ways than one. Like with women, for instance. It's already been mentioned how Riker's careless and carefree shore leave involvement with a woman got him and the Enterprise in trouble in "The Game." But this is apparently an exception as he tends to be more careful than this..

On a more serious personal note, Riker and Deanna Troi were once lovers and were reunited by being posted aboard the Enterprise. Although Riker had been serious about Deanna at one time, he decided that his career was more important to him at this point in his life. But what if he had decided to pursue both? This is what Thomas Riker (Will's double as seen in the aptly named "Second Chances") wants to do. Where the relationship of Thomas Riker and Deanna Troi eventually goes remains to be seen.

Spock, of course, was bound into a marriage contract to T'Pring of Vulcan when he was seven. Years later Spock did his best to delay consummating that contract and finally was released from his bond of honor after entering into pon farr. It turned out that T'Pring already had other plans for her own future which did not include Spock. As far as Spock was concerned, this was just as well. Unlike his father, Sarek, who was married three times, Spock has found his career to be all the consort he needs.

There was a brief romantic encounter with a Romulan during "The Enterprise Incident," but so far as is known this was not one of the reasons Spock undertook his perilous mission to Romulus many years later. Spock's romantic encounters have remained few and far between, perhaps engaging in as many in his lifetime as Will Riker would in an average year.

RIKER AND KIRK?

Riker seemed meant to embody the virile aspects of Kirk. In the early episodes he was the embodiment of the virtues of mankind—strong yet tolerant, intelligent and compassionate, willing to learn from his enemies as well as his friends. He was seen as having no sexual hang-ups, and although it was clear he had once been Deanna Troi's lover, this in no way adversely affected their continuing working relationship and friendship.

The first season made the mistake of having Riker pose too stiffly too often. Additionally, while Jonathan Frakes has an excellent sense of humor, this was not effectively employed until later seasons, making the character seem to take himself and everything else a tad too seriously. The character looks better in his short, trim beard which he has retained since the second season.

Who is the best first officer? Although Riker is more interested in making Starfleet his career, his eyes always seem to be on his next accomplishment. Plus, whether he's a good first officer depends on who his captain is. In "Chain of Command" his substitute captain found Riker to be insubordinate and the worst first officer he'd ever worked with!

Personality plays a large part in how well Riker fits in to his assigned position. When Will Riker was transferred to the Klingon ship The Pagh as part of a temporary officer exchange program, Will demonstrated that he could be as tough as any Klingon and seemed to relish the role.

Spock served on the Enterprise literally for decades, with only a couple years off when Kirk was kicked upstairs and assigned to lecture at Starfleet Academy on Earth. Spock served with distinction for eleven years under Christopher Pike and remained when James T. Kirk replaced him. Unswerving loyalty to Starfleet, coolness under combat conditions and vast deep space experience give Spock the edge here, although it's doubtful he could have made himself fit in comfortably if transferred to a Klingon vessel.

SCIENCE OFFICERS

Data and Spock. Both are science officers. One is an android. The other is a half-human hybrid. Both are superior in their position. Does this mean that the science station is one better assigned to a non-human? While they are no doubt exceptional individuals, a human could certainly be a fine science officer. But science involves cold equations, and who better to appreciate that than an android who cannot feel and a Vulcan who believes that absolute logic is the ultimate accomplishment?

But which Spock are we talking about? Spock's younger years in Starfleet portray a Vulcan who could easily be mistaken for an android. It is for this reason that Data's initial resemblance to Spock went much further than the fact that they both served in the same capacity on their respective versions of the Enterprise.

Spock, in the 23rd century, strove to divest himself of all traces of human emotion. Data, in the 24th century, was created with the absence of emotion and sought to understand the nature of emotion since it sometimes affected the decisions of those around him. He even tried to imitate emotions in order to further explore what it meant to be human, but Data found that imitating something was very different from experiencing it naturally.

MORE SIMILAR THAN DIFFERENT

Spock was often accused of being robot-like, a criticism he would have regarded as a compliment. But as vast and all-encompassing as Spock's memory can be, it cannot touch Data's more perfect and precise total recall. Data was programmed with the complete knowledge of the Federation colony where he was created by Dr. Noonian Soong. His perfect memory allowed Data to pass through Starfleet Academy in record time and be posted to a starship assignment aboard the Trieste as well as other vessels before joining the crew of the newly commissioned Enterprise-D. He is the only android in Starfleet in the 24th century.

Data and Spock both possess great strength. Spock's comes from his Vulcan physique while Data's is mechanical in origin. Spock and Data have both distinguished themselves in the service of Starfleet and have been honored with awards and citations for merit and bravery. They also can both be expected to outlive their comrades in the Enterprise. In Spock's case he lived to meet Data in the 24th century, while Data can be expected to outlive Spock. It is estimated that Sarek was in the neighborhood of 200 earth years when he died but he might well have lived past 250 had he not succumbed to a rare ailment which strikes only Vulcans.

Also on the down side, Spock and Data each have had to deal with an outcast brother. Spock's half-brother, Sybok, rejected the Vulcan ways years before and had left home when Spock was only a small child. Sarek refused to ever speak of Sybok again. Sybok and Spock reconciled shortly before Sybok's death.

Data and his evil twin Lore remained always at odds, although Lore did almost succeed in turning Data to his side when Lore formed an alliance with the Borg.

A THIRST FOR KNOWLEDGE

Data and Spock, as science officers, have a vital interest in discovering the hidden knowledge which is to be found out there on other worlds. Spock further enhances his already vast knowledge with the help of the ship's computer. Since Data is a computer, he tries to apply his knowledge to applicable situations.

When Data became conscious for the first time, his creator had already left. So while the android was sentient, he was not aware of his purpose. Data determined that because he was made in the image of a man, that he should act like a man.

Spock, in following his early pursuit of the Vulcan way, strived to be more like a computer than a man. In this way Spock and Data are complete opposites. In the 24th century, in the "Reunification" incident when Data and Spock met for the first time, Data remarked on this. The android found it remarkable that Spock, who is half-human, tries to be less human while Data, who is an android, wants to achieve what Spock could easily have but resists. As much as Data admired Spock and his accomplishments, he was surprised that the Vulcan would turn his back on what Data may well never be able to achieve—being truly human.

Although an android, Data pursues human interests in his attempt to discover just what being human entails. Besides writing bad poetry, Data also plays the violin. Spock, of course, plays the Vulcan lyre, another string instrument.

The two science officers are more alike than either would care to admit, and both continue to strive to be more than they already are.

THE ENGINEERS

Geordi LaForge initially floundered as the helmsman. Some may have even found it somehow wryly amusing that a blind man was steering the Enterprise. After the first season, one still had no sense of his character. Where there had been a couple of attempts at establishing an engineer, it was only when Geordi was switched to engineering that he began to have any flare, as well as be a character the others would regularly consult. The banana clip visor on his face and his child-like reactions and attitudes didn't help at first. Plus, he seemed more awkward with women than Wesley did, a slightly endearing trait.

LeVar Burton's strength came to the fore slowly as writers began to get a handle on Geordi. His interactions with Starfleet screwup Barclay helped throw his personality into relief. He is obviously good at his job and gets impatient with incompetence, but is also willing to give people a chance or two when prodded. He seems excited by the technobabble he's called upon to recite, and his use of the holodeck to create simulations to explore his engineering ideas is one of the few really intelligent uses of that extraordinary device.

Scotty began as the 23rd century Enterprise engineer and the role grew around him. But while the characters of Kirk, Spock and McCoy deepened, the character of Scotty only broadened. Historically Scotts have been fine engineers, but added to this was a portrayal of Scotty as someone who enjoys his Scotch almost as much as he does caring for his precious "bairns" (the engines) of the Enterprise—maybe even more. The cliche' of Scotty complaining to the captain that he can't give him any more power was an overused one, particularly in the third season of the original STAR TREK.

TWO VERY DIFFERENT ENGINEERS

Scotty was posted as Chief Engineer aboard the first starship named Enterprise. Although it was state-of-the-art for the 23rd century, he would be quite surprised by the changes made when he crossed paths with the 24th century version of the Enterprise—an entirely new starship.

The original Enterprise was charged by dilithium crystals which could wear out and need to be replaced. One of Scotty's functions was to monitor the deterioration of the crystals as well as the balance of the matter-anti-matter pods.

Geordi LaForge is from a very different background than Scotty. While Montgomery Scott grew up in Scotland, Geordi was born in Earth's African Confederation. He had been born blind and his parents accepted his condition. Geordi initially accepted it as well, but was even more dependent on his parents than even the average child is. At the age of 5 the boy suffered a traumatic experience when he was trapped in a burning building where he stood helplessly alone for several minutes until rescued by his parents. It was an experience that even the adult Geordi can still recall in all its horror.

Geordi's parents worked harder than ever after this incident to find some way of helping their son to live a more normal, less handicapped existence. They finally succeeded when the VISOR (Visual Instrument and Sight Organ Replacement) mechanism was developed. This allows Geordi to see on a more advanced wavelength than normal human vision allows.

Besides the advanced starship engines of the 24th century, which can recharge the dilithium crystals, Geordi has other features at his disposal of which Scotty could never have dreamed. The holodeck, through which the computer can create three-dimensional representations of literally anything, allows Geordi to run test programs or even consult with the designer of the warp engines of the Enterprise-D, such as he did in "Booby Trap."

ACROSS THE CENTURY MARK

While the Enterprise of Scotty's time and that of Geordi's are separated by three-quarters of a century, that doesn't mean that the two engineers never had the opportunity to meet. In the incident recorded as "Relics," the Enterprise-D encountered the only known Dyson Sphere—a man made sphere built to encompass a star so that a civilization could be established on the millions of kilometers of area of the sphere.

A transport ship, the Jenolen, was found crashed on it, and inside an operational cycle for a transporter buffer, Geordi and an Away Team reintegrated the pattern of Lt. Commander Montgomery Scott, who had been reported lost in space years before.

Scotty had no way of knowing that 75 years had passed and when he was told that the Enterprise had rescued him, he expected to meet up with Jim Kirk again. He was surprised when told how much time had passed. But his sadness was short-lived when he was able to see the new Enterprise engine room. All of the advances amazed and excited him. But they also confused him. Geordi's initial enthusiasm over meeting the Chief Engineer of the original starship Enterprise soon turned to annoyance as Scotty became bothersome and tried to give advice which was nearly a century out of date.

DIFFERENT PERSONALITY TYPES

Scotty and Geordi may have been engineers, but meeting each other was much like a meeting between a grandfather and a grandson. Scotty waxed eloquent about the good old days while Geordi had to be concerned with the here and now. A personality clash soon developed. Scotty had only a minimal understanding of the warp drive advancements and Geordi didn't have time to deal with retraining someone who once thought he knew it all, and probably had.

It was only after the Enterprise-D was endangered, and Scotty and Geordi were able to pool their skills, that Geordi appreciated Montgomery Scott's innate problem solving talents.

But Geordi was correct when he recognized that he and Scotty are two very different souls. Geordi is not the gregarious, outgoing type that Scotty is. Scott could be the life of the party whereas Geordi was more of the sit in the corner of the party and watch type. And while Scotty could charm the lasses, Geordi was tongue-tied around women—unless they knew a lot about starship engineering. Technology is Geordi's strong suit, not interpersonal relationships. Data often finds it easier to meet and talk to people than Geordi does, perhaps because Data cannot get embarrassed if he says the wrong thing. Geordi is certain that everything he's about to say to a woman will turn out wrong .

Scotty never worries about it as he knows his way around women almost as well as he does around a starship. He loves to regale his shipmates with tall tales as well as entertain them with the bagpipes. But he can turn his musical talent to a serious intent as well such as when he played "Amazing Grace" at Spock's funeral following the "Wrath of Khan" incident. He was as pleased as anyone when Spock was returned to the land of the living.

ENGINEER AND SCIENCE OFFICER

Although Scotty couldn't be called a close friend of Mr. Spock's, they were friends nonetheless. Spock recognized Montgomery Scott's engineering abilities and counted on them when he needed the Enterprise to perform some theoretically possible but completely untried theorem, such as mixing matter and anti-matter cold in "The Naked Time" incident. If there is anyone on the ship who can truly appreciate and understand what the Engineer is capable of, it is the Science Officer.

Spock and Scotty had a more studied, quiet friendship than Kirk and Spock did. While it could be argued that McCoy knew Spock better than Scotty did, during "The Galileo Seven" incident, when McCoy and others continually challenged Spock's command judgment, Scotty stood up for him. Scotty recognized the position Spock was in and the difficulties being brought to bear. And even though Scott was the one who was having to solve the technical problems experienced by the shuttlecraft, he never lost his temper nor blamed Spock for their predicament. Clearly Scotty admired and respected the Enterprise Science Officer.

While Data is capable of even less emotion than Spock, he openly regards Geordi as his closest friend. Whether this is a genuine recognition of all of the inner meanings of friendship, or Data's educated reasoning of what friendship means, is anyone's guess. But Data clearly admires Geordi as both a person and an engineer. Once again the Science Officer recognizes the range of talents exhibited by the ship's engineer.

Conversely, Scotty and Geordi could turn to their respective Science Officers when they needed a leap in logic to go beyond what they knew about possibilities of the technology at their disposal.

Who is the best starship engineer? In the 23rd century, clearly Montgomery Scott was at the top of his field.

In the 24th century, Geordi is still young and learning. He is constantly challenging himself to go beyond the limits of his knowledge, and when he teamed up with Montgomery Scott he learned just how possible that was to achieve.

DOCTORS

Leonard McCoy referred to himself as just "an old country doctor," not that Earth had many of those, if any, in the 23rd century. If anything this was Dr. McCoy yearning for a simpler time when he didn't have to deal with his atoms being scrambled in a transporter beam. As Chief Surgeon on the starship Enterprise in the 23rd century, Dr. McCoy had to deal with problems far beyond what his great, great, great Grandfather would have had to deal with on a world where starship travel was the province of motion pictures. McCoy had to learn Vulcan physiology as well as deal with the problems of aliens who had no human blood.

Dr. Beverly Crusher isn't another "Bones" McCoy, although both are more than competent doctors who care about people. We know she likes to dance (Gates McFadden has a background as a dancer) and worries about her son, as any mother would. She can be forceful or can cozen when it's appropriate, possessing a temper tempered with a real ability to read people. As such, she is one of the most human people on the show but is usually relegated to working in sickbay or underscoring some personal relationship with either Picard or her son, Wesley. Her best episode remains "The Host" where she falls in love with Odan, but can't deal with the parasite's changing of hosts, especially into a new female body.

Deanna Troi was called the ship's counselor but didn't do any counseling until the later episodes. Much was made of her ability as an empath, being able to sense emotions in alien races. However, what she sensed was usually something that was obvious to the audience anyway, making her one of the most consistently boring of the crew until her character received some fine-tuning.

She was initially dressed in what looked like a McDonald's waitress outfit, giving way to a Cosmic Cheerleader outfit. Not that I have anything against cleavage, but her uniform stood out among the others for its differences, which were only amended later. There was no real reason for her being on the bridge except to give the men in the audience something to ogle. Rarely was she given anything of substance to say or do. Some fans of THE NEXT GENERATION remark that they prefer that series because it has more female characters. But Deanna Troi has only infrequently been an improvement over Nurse Chapel's wallflower roles on the original STAR TREK.

THE DEMANDS ON THE DOCTORS

Leonard McCoy and Beverly Crusher are both doctors assigned to ships named Enterprise. Each is an outstanding physician, dedicated to their profession. There the similarities would seem to end—with one notable exception. They both fervently believe that their most important duty is their stewardship of the captain's health.

Complicating that duty was the relationship each had with their captain. Kirk, along with Spock, was McCoy's best friend, and he had a tendency to overstep the boundaries of protocol, a habit that both irritated and frustrated Kirk. This bothered McCoy not at all, for as a doctor he considered himself outside the pale of the ship's hierarchy and was prone to say what he pleased. In spite of the military ranks many of the characters on STAR TREK have, the doctors have consistently been portrayed as having no rank.

This is a result of Starfleet being portrayed as a quasi-military organization in that it looks like the military but it isn't really. This was Gene Roddenberry's attempt to create an organized atmosphere while serving his pasificist side as well.

Beverly Crusher's friendship with Picard wasn't the normal Captain—Chief Medical Officer relationship either. Picard and Crusher are probably semi in love with each other, but they keep their emotions firmly submerged and simply enjoy each other's company. Her behavior, however, never bordered on the insubordinate as McCoy's sometimes did, with one exception. In the episode "Suspicion" she defied Starfleet regulations and Picard's orders and was on the verge of being expelled from the service as a result—until she was proven right. So Beverly could be as headstrong as Leonard McCoy given sufficient provocation. It just seemed to come more easily and quickly to McCoy. It was second nature to him.

These friendships between doctor and captain made for some interesting confrontations when the doctors felt their commanding officer was too ill, or too badly injured, to be on duty. There were times when Kirk and Picard would grumble, to anyone who would listen, that ship's doctors were frequently entirely too dedicated.

When McCoy had to confront a stubborn Kirk, his only ally was Spock, a man of science, but not medicine. Crusher was more fortunate. She had Counselor Deanna Troi to back her when she felt Picard should be in sickbay rather than on the bridge. Otherwise, trying to equate these two doctors is like comparing apples and oranges.

THE SHIP'S COUNSELOR

As Starfleet and the Federation extended their journeys further into space, training the crews became more costly and missions longer. This created problems when crew members, unhappy at being separated from families, either resigned, requested shore duty, or assignments on ships with shorter missions.

To combat the financial losses expended on officers who resigned, and maintain experienced crews for the long missions, Starfleet introduced two new programs—ships equipped with family quarters, and a ship's counselor. One of the first of these counselors was half Betazoid/half human Deanna Troi.

McCoy had retired before these changes were made. When confronted with a crew member suffering with the stress of long years in space, trauma after a battle or just plain fatigue, he had to use what little space-psychiatry training he'd had, coupled with medication, physical therapy, and gut instinct.

JAMES
DOOHAN

Sometimes these methods worked and sometimes they didn't. McCoy would rage within himself at these failures.

During the twenty-seven years McCoy served on the first two ships named Enterprise, he would have welcomed the assistance of a Deanna Troi as he struggled through a counseling session with a distraught patient.

LIFE ABOARD THE ENTERPRISE

Another source of frustration was McCoy's lack of knowledge concerning the anatomy of the many aliens he was forced to treat. Circumstances forced him into what he referred to as on-the-job-training when Spock needed medical attention. He felt equally thwarted when confronted with an injured, previously unknown species.

McCoy believed he had executed a major coup when he lured Dr. M'Benga, an expert in the treatment of Vulcans and other aliens, away from a Vulcan medical facility to serve on the Enterprise. Officially he was McCoy's assistant, but M'Benga understood that his number one priority was Spock. Even a hangnail was to be taken seriously. As much as McCoy hated to admit it at times, he knew the ship ran smoother with a healthy Spock on the bridge.

When McCoy was called back to active duty during the V'ger emergency, he was happy to find that Christine Chapel, his former nurse, had earned her medical degree—a degree which included alien anatomy, and that she was once again serving on the Enterprise.

By the time Beverly Crusher began her medical studies decades later, great strides had been made in the study of alien cultures. Before she even received her degree she had more knowledge on treating the many species she would meet in space than McCoy had after all his years of service.

CRUSHER AND TROI: TEAMMATES

Dr. Crusher also had the benefit of Counselor Troi's abilities. If An injured crewman insisted they felt fine, a gesture from Troi would indicate if the crewman was being completely honest. The doctor considers herself very fortunate to have Troi, and feels doubly blessed to have a Betazoid telepath, even if she is half human.

Troi is a ship's counselor rather than a physician. However she is knowledgeable in some of the medical disciplincs. She is also a graduate of Starfleet Academy Command School, although this is not a requirement for ship's counselors. She carries the rank of Lieutenant Commander.

Deanna Troi insisted on following in her deceased father's footsteps with a career in Starfleet, much against her mother, Lwaxana Troi's, wishes. Lwaxana wanted to see her daughter married, preferably to ". . . that nice Commander Riker. . . ," and happily producing children.

As a descendent of royalty, Deanna is a member of one of the richest and most powerful families on Betazed, but she has never been able to convince her mother that she is happy with her Starfleet career.

Lwaxana's marriage to a Terran had the effect of reducing the usual strong Betazoid telepathic powers that Deanna inherited to the lesser ability of detecting moods and emotions. She cannot determine exactly the words another is thinking but she can detect if someone is being evasive or outright lying. In addition to counseling crew members, her duties also include advising the captain of the intentions of beings with whom they come in contact.

CRUSHER AND McCOY

McCoy, a native of Georgia in Earth's old North America, came from a long line of doctors. He was married soon after he graduated from medical school and had a daughter, Joanna. The marriage was a disaster, and to escape from his problems, McCoy joined Starfleet, taking his daughter with him. She eventually went to live with McCoy's sister and brother-in-law on Centaurus. Father and daughter saw each other only on those rare occasions when the Enterprise was in the vicinity.

Beverly Crusher, the daughter of Paul and Isabel Howard, was born in Copernicus on Luna. She married Starfleet Commander Jack Crusher and had a son, Wesley. Jack was serving on the Stargazer under the command of his close friend, Captain Jean-Luc Picard, when he was killed while leading an

Away Team. When Beverly completed her medical degree she enlisted in Starfleet and was eventually assigned the Enterprise, at her request. History seemed to be repeating itself, for once again an officer named Crusher was serving under a Captain named Picard.

Shortly after Beverly Crusher was posted to the Enterprise, 137 year old Dr. McCoy visited the outpost where the Enterprise was docked. Whether the 23rd century Chief Surgeon of the Enterprise met his 24th century counterpart was never recorded. What was recorded was that McCoy still hated to use the transporter.

Crusher and McCoy did work together after the fact in the incident known as "The Naked Now." When the crew of the Enterprise-D began suffering from a mysterious malady such as had once stricken the 23rd century Enterprise, Dr. Crusher found McCoy's log and his cure recorded in the ship's computer. While McCoy's original cure didn't work on this altered version of the ailment, it pointed Beverly in the right direction to discover the remedy for the 24th century incarnation of space madness.

SPACE MEDICINE

In the 23rd century, intersteller exploration was still in its early days. While many new worlds and civilizations had been discovered, many more were still to be found. Space medicine was in its infancy as well, but Dr. McCoy was on the cutting edge, striving to discover the seemingly undiscoverable. In the incident recorded as "Devil in the Dark," McCoy had to decide on an intelligent treatment for a silicon based, non-human life form which had been injured by phaser fire. He succeeded using a silicon based cement. Even McCoy was amazed, exclaiming, "By golly, Jim, I'm beginning to think I can cure a rainy day!"

While xenomorphic medicine had advanced considerably by Beverly Crusher's time, she had much to discover as well. Vulcan physiology wasn't the mystery it had been in McCoy's time, but Klingon biology was an area which had been little explored. On the Klingon homeworld, treatments for illness or injury were minimal as that culture believed in killing the weak. In that warrior culture it was considered dishonorable to become a burden.

A crippled Klingon would commit suicide rather than endure life as less than a full bodied warrior. With attitudes like that, little had been done in the realm of Klingon medicine since they would just as soon kill rather than try to find a cure for a debilitating condition.

Beverly Crusher encountered this inexplicable philosophy when Worf was crippled in an accident aboard the Enterprise. His spine crushed, the Klingon knew he would never achieve full mobility again. Rather than gain only minimal body movement and become an object of pity, Worf preferred death. Beverly was beside herself as Worf could not be reasoned with. When Dr. Toby Russell, a visiting neuro-geneticist, suggested an experimental treatment, Beverly resisted. But Russell disregarded Crusher's advisory and presented the possibilities to Worf. Due to the little understood physiology of Klingons, the operation proved to be a success and more was discovered about Klingon biology than the Klingons had ever tried to learn about themselves.

McCoy engaged a similarly risky surgery when he had to transplant Spock's brain back into his head and reconnect the countless nerve endings. An education computer on an alien world gave McCoy the knowledge he needed to accomplish this miraculous feat, but what he learned was implanted to last only a short time. As the knowledge faded he had to use his own skills and judgment, as well as Spock's suggestions since the Vulcan remained conscious throughout the surgery. There is no indication that brain surgery of that order has been discovered by Federation technology even in the 24th century.

THE TWO DOCTORS

Crusher and McCoy are at the top of their fields for their time. While McCoy calls himself an old country doctor, he is actually less conservative about experimenting medically than his 24th century counterpart is. When McCoy determines that he's deficient in some area he moves forward to unlock the door which bars his way.

Beverly Crusher is part of a starship society in which the Federation is not so distant and out of reach as it was in McCoy's time. The Enterprise-D is generally within a day's travel of an established Federation colony. The original starship Enterprise was sometimes weeks away from the nearest starbase. When you're far from home you improvise, and Dr. McCoy became a master of that. But Beverly resists improvising if it could put someone's life in danger, citing her medical ethics. Comparing the two circumstances is much like comparing life in wartime and life in peacetime.

Leonard McCoy was at war with the limited knowledge he had of alien biology. Beverly Crusher believes that one should err on the side of caution, even if it means that it pushes a discovery back several years. There is something to be said for each philosophy as circumstances dictate need. Worf preferred death to a disability and so Beverly Crusher reluctantly complied even though it went against everything she believed.

When McCoy and his comrades were infected with a potentially fatal disease in the "Miri" incident, he performed the ultimate in human experimentation—he injected himself with the experimental cure. Would Beverly Crusher have done this? Perhaps. But she is not as willing to take the risks that McCoy took. Beverly Crusher is thus the more ethical physician, but Dr. McCoy is the more adventurous one with more discoveries to his credit.

Ethics are certainly important to a physician and it would be interesting to see Crusher and McCoy debate their interpretations of the Hippocratic Oath. It would be a lively and intelligent debate to be sure.

SECONDARY BRIDGE CREWS

As the starships grew bigger and better over the years, the duties of the crew saw many changes. Some positions were eliminated, others combined, and new ones added. Most early bridge officers filled one position. However, all were required to have a working knowledge of all bridge stations, and to be able to quickly man any station should an emergency arise.

Some captains, such as Kirk, enjoyed the advantages of commanding the same crew for decades. Others had frequent changes, perhaps an entire crew. And a few, such as Picard, were fortunate to have to make only an occasional change.

The flagship of the fleet, always named Enterprise, usually experienced less turnover among personnel than did other ships. It was considered the highest honor, perhaps the pinnacle of one's career, to be selected to serve on the Enterprise. And only the very best were chosen. The following are a few more of those "best."

UHURA AND WORF

The only person to serve as Kirk's communications officer on the original Enterprise was Lieutenant Nyota Uhura. Of course there were other officers who served during the alternate shifts, or on the rare occasions when Uhura was assigned to a landing party, but during any critical situation, Nyota was the person Kirk wanted at that station.

Uhura's counterpart on the Enterprise 1701-D, Lieutenant Worf, is, ironically, a Klingon. Worf, the only Klingon to serve as a Starfleet officer, has numerous duties in addition to communications. He is responsible for shields, for firing the ship's weapons and is the Enterprise security officer.

Uhura was an expert at understanding, and interpreting, obscure languages. Codes was another field in which she excelled. If another world developed a code that she couldn't break, it was unlikely that anyone, with the possible exception of Spock, could do so.

Frustrated that the Klingons had managed to break three of the Federation's codes in as many months, Uhura designed a code that was not only Klingon proof, but thwarted the code-breaking attempts of all other worlds.

Remembering her Earth history, she recalled that during World War II, the Allied Forces in the South Pacific were having the same problems with their codes. They solved that difficulty by bringing in members of the Navajo Indian Nation of the southwest United States to be deployed as "Code Talkers," to serve as coast-watchers, and operate military radios. Their language was so difficult that few people in the world, including other tribes, could speak it, and it had never been heard by the enemy. The ploy had been successful and suggested a possible solution to her problem.

Born in the Confederation of Africa, Uhura decided to develop a code using certain words from her people's ancient Swahili dialect. This code was so successful that even the universal translator could not accurately decipher the correct definitions of most of the words. One wonders if Worf employs her Swahili code on the 24th century Enterprise, and what Uhura would think of that?

SKILLS LEAD TO PROMOTIONS

Uhura had more than her share of close calls and wild adventures, and on too many occasions found herself staring death in the face. Many of these events pale when compared with those of Worf. She never had any reason to doubt where her loyalties should be. Worf, on the other hand, was a product of two worlds—peace loving Earth and the warrior class society of the Klingon Empire.

Worf had been serving under Lieutenant Tasha Yar, who filled the positions mentioned above. When she was killed on Vagra II, Picard appointed Worf as acting security chief. A few weeks later he was promoted to Lieutenant and permanently replaced Yar.

During the years the Enterprise was in dry-dock, Uhura was promoted to Lieutenant Commander and served at Starfleet Command. She was more than happy to leave that position when Admiral Kirk needed her on his galaxy-saving expeditions.

PECULIAR TALENTS

Born on the Klingon homeworld of Qo'noS, Worf, the son of Mogh, was orphaned at age six during the Romulan massacre at Khitomer. He was found, and later adopted, by Starfleet officer Sergey Rozhenko and his wife Helena. They lived on Gault for a time before moving to Earth, where Worf grew up along with his human stepbrother.

Worf and his stepbrother entered the Starfleet Academy together, but the brother was unhappy and soon ended his studies. After serving on the Enterprise for several years, Worf learned he has a younger brother, Kurn, who was not with the family at Khitomer.

One particular special duty that Worf was called upon to perform would have been a welcome one for Uhura, but not for the Klingon. During a disaster on the ship, Keiko O'Brien went into labor and Worf, a very reluctant hero, delivered the child since he had studied how to do it on the computer. But Worf never considered being a midwife one of his special talents.

Among Uhura's many talents is the ability to completely dismantle her station and return it to top working conditions. If an enemy believed he could gain advantage during battle by destroying the communications system, he obviously was not familiar with the Enterprise communications officer.

A talented singer and musician, Uhura entertained the crew during her leisure hours and has even been known to distract an enemy with her dancing and singing.

THE KLINGON WAY

Worf began to dominate as more stories focused on his differences with the other crew members. Initially he could predictably be counted on to advise "attack," which almost never seemed to be taken seriously as an option if he did so. In most respects, however, Worf simply isn't different enough. He seems like an overly aggressive human most of the time rather than someone truly alien.

Curiously, the episode "Family" revealed that Worf had been raised by Russian-Jewish parents, and yet there has never been before or since the slightest hint that Worf has been influenced by his adoptive parents' culture. (Not that he had to offer matzoh balls and chicken soup to someone who was sick, but surely something of his parents should have been incorporated into his character.)

It broke a minor taboo about TV heroes when Worf refused to donate his blood to save a dying Romulan, which gave that particular episode a little more edge, but the character's racism is rarely explored. More disturbing is that Worf, after being acclimated to the peaceful ideals of Starfleet Academy and serving the Federation for so long, finds the concept of peaceful Klingons abhorrent when he encounters them in "Birthright."

Here he becomes a proponent of preserving even the negative aspects about his culture rather than redefining just what a warrior is. Couldn't he conceive of a warrior being someone who struggles for justice rather than someone who kills enemies and gives the blood cry? Haven't his experiences in Starfleet influenced his outlook in any way?

Worf and Uhura are as opposite as can be, for the most part. Worf is a warrior and lives this philosophy first and foremost. While Uhura is not one to normally engage in a battle physically, she proved she could take care of herself in the "Mirror, Mirror" incident when she pulled a knife on the sinister, alternate universe version of Lt. Sulu and made it clear that she would fight him if pushed. Worf would have admired that gesture greatly.

THE HELMSMEN

Captain Kirk never met Commander Data, but being the kind of man, the kind of captain he was, it is unlikely that he would have selected the android over Lieutenant Sulu as his helmsman.

Sulu came onto the ship as a staff physicist. When an emergency arose and the helmsman was injured, Sulu was ordered to take his place. After the space-dust had cleared, so to speak, Kirk realized that his substitute helmsman had executed a maneuver that pulled them out of the path of an on-rushing ship bent on committing suicide and taking the Enterprise along with them. Sulu's days in the medical field were over, and he went on to become one of Kirk's most valued officers.

Commander Data is the regular helmsman for the Enterprise 1701-D. However, his many other duties frequently take him away from the helm. As an android possessing super-human abilities, it is hardly fair to compare him with lesser beings, but as Data himself will admit, there are many things humans can do that he cannot.

It is unlikely if he will ever acquire the gut-instinct that some people seem to be born with. But Data is ideal for this position, for his ability to calculate all possibilities, then act upon them at the same instant, make the android the ideal helmsman. Picard, Riker and the rest of the crew share a feeling of well-being when Data is at his post.

MAN AND SUPERMAN

The San Francisco native, Hikaru Sulu, originally decided on a career in physics because he loved the field of science and enjoyed working with energy. But in the depths of his mind he had a vision—a vision of himself in command of a great starship. He also believed the field of science was a more realistic goal, until Kirk ordered him to take the helmsman's chair that fateful day. From that moment on he never wavered in his dream of commanding a ship of his own.

Like Sulu, Data also believes he is a prime candidate for his own command. There are many, from both Starfleet Command and the people who would be serving under him, who believe that an android should not be placed in command of a ship. He has proven many times on the Enterprise that he does have that ability, but it wasn't until the Romulans attempted to interfere with the civil strife within the Klingon Empire, that Data was able to prove his ability as a captain on his own ship.

Fearing a Romulan victory would end the peace between the Federation and Klingon Empire, Picard deployed a fleet of ships along the route the Romulans would have to take. Data was appointed Captain of the Sutherland, and despite a near insubordinate first officer, and a reluctant crew, Data found a method to detect the cloaked Romulan ships and end the threat.

Sulu would serve alongside James Kirk for many years before his dream at last became a reality and he was given command of the starship Excelsior. His life came full circle when his first mission, a three year science research expedition in the Beta quadrant, coupled first love science, with his dream. He didn't expect a hero's welcome when he returned from such a routine mission, however he arrived just in time to help Kirk and his former ship prevent conspirators from their attempts to sabotage the Klingon Peace Conference at Khitomer. Along with Kirk and the Enterprise, Sulu and the Excelsior received that hero's welcome.

COMMAND DECISIONS

Sulu and Data both had an early taste of what it was like to be in command. When Sulu, the physicist, was yanked onto the helm in an emergency, he experienced what it was like to be in control of a starship. It was a sensation he couldn't walk away from, only continue walking towards.

Data does not have an emotional link to be a starship commander as his interests lie elsewhere. Basically Data is more concerned in being the best at whatever his assignment is. When he was placed in command of a starship in "Redemption," he used his artificial intellect along with the skills he had picked up watching Captain Picard and Commander Riker at their duty posts. Commanding a starship requires not just knowledge, but experience. In Data's case he chose to disobey orders when he determined that to follow them would be an error. It was the kind of educated command decision Picard might well have made. It could be argued that the android made a "gut" decision.

Perhaps like Captain Sulu, Data too will earn his captain's pips.

THE NAVIGATORS

During a stop at a distant starbase early in the second year of his first five year mission, Captain Kirk welcomed aboard several new crew members. One of these was a young man newly graduated from Starfleet Academy—Ensign Pavel Chekov.

As a trainee, he temporarily filled many positions, both on and off the bridge. Long before the end of his probationary period, both Kirk and Spock believed that the young ensign's talents were at the navigation console where he also served as weapons officer.

This was a relief for Kirk who had tried several officers at the post. Lieutenants Stiles, Kelso and Farrell had all taken their turns as navigators. While they were all good officers, it wasn't until Chekov came along that Kirk was satisfied that he had the right man.

Chekov had some big shoes to fill, as the position had once been very capably filled by Kirk's close friend, Gary Mitchell, who died in the line of duty.

Jean-Luc Picard has not had the good fortune that Kirk enjoyed in selecting a navigator. After Wesley Crusher was appointed an Acting Ensign, he filled the position well until he left the Enterprise to enter Starfleet Academy. Since then, Riker has assigned a number of officers to the post, but they were either hurt in battle, proved unsatisfactory, or transferred off the Enterprise.

ENSIGNS

Chekov proved himself well as a navigator and was called back to serve on the reconditioned Enterprise for the V'ger incident. This was even before anyone knew that Kirk would be back in his old position in the center seat. Chekov's deep space experience served him in good stead on this mission, and he distinguished himself so well that he accepted a promotion to the science ship Reliant.

On the Enterprise-D, the navigator who showed the most promise was Ensign Ro Laren, a Bajoran who had begun her career with eyes on a captain's chair. She had rapidly moved up the chain of command, gaining the rank of Lieutenant Commander and was second officer on the Wellington. During a battle on Garon II, eight crew members of an Away Team, under Ro's command, were killed. She was court martialed and sentenced to prison.

Several years later, Admiral Kennelly offered her a pardon if she would assist in a mission involving Bajoran terrorists. She agreed but soon learned that the Admiral had his own reasons for wanting her help, and she rebelled. When Kennelly was exposed, Ro was exonerated of any wrong doing. Picard offered her a post on the Enterprise, against Riker's wishes. She accepted and served as navigator, regaining some of her early promise.

While Chekov fit in well with the bridge crew on the 23rd century Enterprise, Ro Laren wasn't quite so affable on the 24th century counterpart of the Federation flagship. Still smarting from her treatment at the hands of Starfleet, she is not afraid to challenge orders or question the wisdom of a command decision. The commands she usually questions are those given by Lt. Riker.

Chekov was rotated back to the Enterprise when the Reliant was hijacked and lost in a battle with the Enterprise. But Ensign Chekov enjoyed returning to his position of navigator on the Enterprise. He felt at home.

Ro Laren's home was Bajor, and when the Cardassians ended their occupation of that world, Ensign Ro left the Enterprise to resume her life there. For her, Starfleet had been a means to an end and with Bajor free it was time to return to the life she truly loved. For Chekov, the Enterprise was the life he loved and that's where he chose to remain.

In the end, it always comes back to the Enterprise. The focal point. The arrow pointed at heaven. A society among the stars.

CHAPTER 4

COMPARING TREKS

Now it's time to go head to head. In this corner, weighing in at 79 episodes and 6 movies is Trek Classic. In that corner, weighing in at 150 episodes and counting is TNG.

"We grew beyond the original show.
We love the original and those actors,
but we see the world differently now
and our show reflects that."
Gene Roddenberry
USA TODAY, November 1, 1990

When STAR TREK premiered in 1966, there was not an abundance of science fiction on television. Unfortunately, other than the anthology series such as TWILIGHT ZONE and OUTER LIMITS, in those days futuristic series with continuing characters seemed to be the arena solely of producer Irwin Allen. Allen had a knack for making an outstanding pilot episode and then quickly running out of ideas and recycling plots, props, sets and basically dumbing everything down quickly. LOST IN SPACE did not start out as a children's show but within a dozen episodes had become one.

Gene Roddenberry hadn't produced a science fiction series before. He'd produced THE LIEUTENANT and had been head writer on HAVE GUN WILL TRAVEL. But STAR TREK came

GENE RODDENBERRY AND HIS TWO CAPTAINS, WILLIAM SHATNER AND PATRICK STEWART AT THE JUNE 6, 1991 25TH ANNIVERSARY STAR TREK BASH.

**DEFOREST
KELLEY
AND
JAMES
DOOHAN**

out of a lifelong interest in science fiction and a desire to see it done well.

Fans were introduced to Kirk, Spock, McCoy and the grand starship Enterprise on Sept. 8, 1966 with "The Man Trap," written by George Clayton Johnson. This was not the first episode filmed, though. What often happens is that when a new series is set to air, the network will look at the episodes completed prior to the premiere date and choose the one they think will get the series off with a bang. Strangely enough, the episode chosen, while certainly dramatic, is far more traditional in its approach to televised science fiction than much of what followed.

In 1986, Roddenberry was asked to repeat himself, to try to "Catch lightning in a bottle twice," as Leonard Nimoy described the challenge of creating a second STAR TREK. "When Paramount originally approached me to do a new series, I turned them down," Roddenberry explained. "I did not want to devote the tremendous amount of time necessary to producing another show. In order to keep the original series going, I practically had to disown my daughters. I had no time for them when they were school age. I did not want to do that to my life again. There is only one way I know to write and produce and that is to throw my energy at the project all the time. So when they began to think about a second series, I said I would not do it. Then they said, 'Well, suppose we figure a way that it could be done so you would be in charge?' I thought they were kidding. The studio said that I could be in full control of the creative standard. I asked a few questions, and they said, 'Yeah, sure, you must know these things because you've been doing them anyway under network guidance.'

"I told the studio that if they went the syndication route, I would go for it. Not only would I go for it, I would go for it full blast. I told them I would find ways of doing STAR TREK that would give them extra elements. I think we have done that." A STAR TREK series would be launched with an all new cast, set seventy-five years after the original series, and featuring the Enterprise of that farther future, the NCC 1701-D. Paramount was banking that a syndicated show would generate revenues. It seemed impossible. But Gene Roddenberry worked hard to produce a new STAR TREK which would be true to the ideals of the original and still have its own flavor.

THE FIRST SEASONS

Both the original STAR TREK and it's modern spin-off took their time establishing the characters and concentrating on telling stories which would include interesting snippets of characterization. When the episode "The Man Trap" was first broadcast, Trek Classic actually established Dr. McCoy more fully than any of the other characters. From the structure of "The Man Trap," one would have thought that Dr. McCoy was the main character. It was the only episode focusing largely on McCoy which appeared in the first season, and it became the introductory show for the series.

With the focus on Dr. McCoy we get an off-center view of STAR TREK. Everything which happens in "The Man Trap" ultimately impacts on McCoy in some manner. The planet they visit has his old girlfriend, Nancy, living with her husband, Prof. Crater. McCoy and Nancy had almost gotten married years before but she chose Crater over McCoy. Bones is clearly happy to see her again and refuses to believe anything bad about her, particularly the suggestion that she could be responsible for some mysterious deaths. When the salt vampire appears to McCoy in the form of Nancy, it plays on his sympathies and then assumes his form in order to move about the ship undetected.

While many people discuss the meteoric rise in popularity of Mr. Spock, Dr. McCoy was no slouch either. There are many Classic Trek fans who actually find McCoy more interesting than Kirk or Spock. DeForest Kelley is only about ten years older than his co-stars but he nevertheless projected the air of a father figure, even in 1966. He was wise as well as protective of people, and when he'd get into an argument, his emotions rose out of his concern for others far more than out of any selfish motivations. McCoy was always the selfless physician, giving of himself for the betterment of his fellow man. He was the conscience of STAR TREK.

20 YEARS LATER

When Gene Roddenberry was asked what he thought of the scripts for the first season of THE NEXT GENERATION, he replied, "We got some good writing in the old series, and we've had some good writing in the new series. But most of the writing comes from a very few, very good people who labor hard, and very often they are staff people.

"In the first STAR TREK, I rewrote or heavily polished the first thirteen episodes so that Mr. Spock would be the Mr. Spock that I had in my mind. This was enormous labor. Then this began to catch on and we got some good writers on this.

"In STAR TREK—THE NEXT GENERATION, I rewrote thirteen episodes. I don't want to act out a big I did this, I did that, but as far as the basic original writing, I had to do that again, with few exceptions. It is the way episodic television is. Now as the year has gone on, I've found some good people and I hope to find more. I would stand in the driving rain for a good writer. It's not a question of who you know. I just need someone who does good work."

While your average TV series sets up a premise and repeats it week after week, with little variation in character or structure, TNG was not your average show. With an ensemble cast, on a superficial level it could be compared with shows like HILL STREET BLUES, ST. ELSEWHERE or L.A. LAW where we could see a lot of characters vying for attention while the series sought to stabilize and achieve a balance. Early on it seemed that while all of the characters were getting some attention, there was no focal point. This was finally achieved when Picard and Riker emerged as the main characters.

INTRODUCTIONS

When a series begins, it has to establish who its characters are. Certainly we can tell them apart quickly enough by appearance, but we have to be able to tell their personalities apart as well. Nothing is more boring than a group of characters who speak as though they're the product of a hive mind wherein they all have interchangeable dialogue.

I can still recall when I first saw the show in 1966 and thinking that it wasn't bad, but I wasn't on fire about it. Not yet. "The Man Trap" was a routine story which, while certainly well done, would have worked better had it aired a few weeks later after the rest of the characters had been better established.

In the second episode, "Charlie X," the basic humanism in the series emerged. Although Kirk's plea fell on deaf ears, his sense of compassion had been clearly established.

The third episode shown was the STAR TREK pilot, "Where No Man Has Gone Before," and this went much further in establishing the characterizations of Kirk and Spock. Although Spock was a super-Vulcan in this story, demonstrating coldly calculated logic when he advised Kirk to kill his old friend Gary Mitchell, other sides are shown as well. Because Mitchell was an old classmate of Kirk's, references are made to his days at Starfleet Academy, filling in more bits of Kirk's background. By the time the episode ended, we had a firm idea of just who Kirk and Spock were and the relationship of their character dynamics.

"Where No Man Has Gone Before" is a rousing story of fantastic adventure which explores the limits of how humanity is measured. It is heavy on action-adventure, and even climaxes in the kind of long, drawn-out fist-fights common to adventure shows of that period. And yet the action is placed in a human context from start to finish. It could be said that there are no villains in that episode, just victims. STAR TREK showed that willingness to stretch its scripts with the addition of such character complexities early in its first season.

TOUGH VOYAGING

One would have thought that Roddenberry wouldn't have found it that difficult to introduce the characters in his STAR TREK spin-off, THE NEXT GENERATION. He just needed to tell a strong story, such as "Where No Man Has Gone Before" did, and use it to reveal who the characters are within the demands of the dramatic setting. But it didn't work out that way. It was as though Roddenberry had forgotten much of what he had learned while inadvertently repeating himself in the wrong ways.

Launching THE NEXT GENERATION with a much ballyhooed two hour adventure, "Encounter At Farpoint," was a good idea, unfortunately the script wasn't up to the challenge. The story careened back and forth between two virtually unrelated plotlines—the intervention of the obnoxious, self-important "Q" and the mystery at Farpoint Station.

When I later learned that Fontana had written a script dealing with the Farpoint mystery and Roddenberry added the Q storyline himself and forced them together, I could see why I felt as I did when watching it. The story tries hard to introduce all of the characters while really revealing little about them, other than Picard's willingness to surrender in situations where Kirk would have defied the odds.

From the start Q was a virtual clone of Trelane, the all powerful alien child from the Trek Classic episode "Squire Of Gothos." In fact the portrayal of Trelane's parents at the end of that old episode is in keeping with what the race from which "Q" comes from are really like. Trelane's parents were portrayed as all-powerful, disembodied entities from a previously unknown alien race. Trelane had taken human form merely to play games with the Enterprise crew, just as Q adopts a human form to harass the Enterprise-D.

While demonstrating that Picard and Kirk are very different, "Encounter At Farpoint" forced a comparison that was not in Picard's favor. The story lurched back and forth, introducing new ideas, such as the families on the Enterprise, and then demonstrating what a horrible idea that is when the ship has to perform a saucer separation in order to remove the families from the main vessel being threatened by Q. The episode actually would have been more interesting had Q gone after the part of the ship with the families and ignored Picard. While the ending with the interplanetary jellyfish is touching and wrought with some beautiful special effects, it seems to be an attempt to distract us and leave us with a warm feeling about the show. Instead we were left with the feeling that we were watching a work in progress and that even Roddenberry didn't know who all of his characters really were.

THE NAKED ID

In the '60s, Roddenberry correctly surmised that a show with several characters, particularly one which demanded more of its audience such as a science fiction series did, needed to establish its background as clearly as possible. In the original STAR TREK this was accomplished in "The Naked Time," a dramatic tale which dealt with the inner feelings of many of the characters on the series, including the strangely aloof Mr. Spock.

In this episode, Spock's friendship with Kirk is explored and the Vulcan reveals that the philosophy of his people prevented him from ever telling his mother that he loved her. The humanity beneath the studied veneer of the half-Vulcan science officer came exploding to the surface under the effects of the alien virus. The twist is that it didn't make a person insane so much as it forced them to confront what was in their psyche. It was like an involuntary group therapy session or how a person might react when given truth serum.

The exception is Christine Chapel. When she confesses her love for Spock to him, she is not upset but in fact actually appears to be happy. She may well have hoped that Spock would respond to her. Even before this I had become fascinated with the character of Spock. He had clearly been included as the important alien element in this science fiction series, and was there as a constant reminder that this was the realm of the future. Spock quickly became an integral factor in the storm of popularity which overtook the series. Each succeeding episode only re-established this. Even though Spock was still just a major supporting character in these early stories, he was soon to emerge as a very solid co-star of STAR TREK.

THE NEXT GENERATION tried to repeat this concept of character exploration in "The Naked Now," written by J. Michael Bingham, from a story by John D.F. Black and J. Michael Bingham. Black worked on the Trek Classic episode "The Naked Time," but going back to the author of the story you're writing a sequel to doesn't necessarily mean that it will be handled well.

The original story examined feelings that were not apparent beneath the surface, with many of the character traits revealed having dramatic as well as tragic overtones. Drama is ignored in this sequel in lieu of characters acting crazy. For instance, Tasha Yar seduces Data, while Wesley causes the Enterprise to be put in jeopardy (which was an undercurrent in the original, but seemingly the main plot in this sequel). Wesley Crusher is given his first opportunity to save the Enterprise here, but then that's only reasonable since it's his fault that it's in danger here at all!

Some of the actors on the show, such as Jonathan Frakes, felt that it was too early to have the bridge crew acting out of character since the viewers still weren't sure who the characters were. He's right, but for the wrong reason. The point of "The Naked Time" was never to have characters act strangely but rather to have them reveal what they are really like inside and what their private demons are like. In this way the characters were broadened and deepened. They weren't supposed to be acting crazy, just completely uninhibited. In "The Naked Now" they acted crazy.

DOUBLE TROUBLE

Like many classic episodes of STAR TREK, "The Enemy Within" has taken on a virtually archetypal quality with the passage of time. Kirk's split into good and evil almost seems a cliché at first, primarily because the basic dilemma of guessing which one is the hero, and which the villain, has been repeated endlessly on many television programs. William Shatner's over-the-top performance as the two halves of James Kirk certainly contributes to this view of "The Enemy Within." But on closer examination it turns out to be quite a memorable episode.

"The Enemy Within" was scripted by Richard Matheson, one of the best writers ever to work in television. Matheson is probably best known for his numerous TWILIGHT ZONE episodes, which include "Nightmare At 20,000 Feet," which featured a pre-TREK appearance by the young William Shatner. In Matheson's hands, the science fiction gag of having a transporter malfunction create duplicate Kirks becomes a vehicle for an intriguing examination of the elements that make up a man's personality. The director for this episode was Leo Penn.

In "The Enemy Within," the crisis is triggered when a crewman bearing traces of an alien metal beams up from the planet Alpha 177. The resulting distortion in the basic transporter functions has a drastic effect on the next man who beams up, who just happens to be Captain James T. Kirk. It takes awhile for the problem to become obvious to anyone. The evil Kirk created by the malfunction is as cunning as he is strong-willed, which enables him to pass himself off as the original for quite some time.

The good Kirk, unfortunately, has not retained any of the energy or motivation which inspires the evil Kirk. Even after the problem is discovered and the evil Kirk apprehended, no solution is immediately apparent. The evil Kirk has nothing but contempt for his counterpart. The good Kirk has little to offer in the way of leadership qualities, and becomes even more ineffective as the effects of the split begin to weaken both Kirks, with potentially fatal results for the evil Captain.

DUAL PERSONALITIES

As the dual Kirks spiral toward their fates, efforts to decontaminate the transporter go on, monopolizing Scotty's time. The rest of the landing party is still on the planet below, enduring freezing conditions with no hope of rescue. Scotty's work goes on, but the transporter consistently splits anything, living or dead, that goes through it. Scotty finally manages to reverse the problem, but a small alien creature (actually a small dog made up to look alien) which was split, does not survive its reintegration. Finally, the two Kirks, realizing that they will die anyway as separate entities, decide to go ahead and the reintegration is a success. The landing party is rescued in time, and the Enterprise goes along its way, with a restored Jim Kirk at the helm.

This is certainly a highly representative episode of STAR TREK, replete with a dual performance which could only have been acted by William Shatner. Matheson's theme elevates the story far above the basic crisis of distinguishing one Kirk from the other. The dramatic tension is heightened by the need for the two Kirks to realize that their lives can only continue by being joined, rather than by battling it out to a typical "you-or-me" conclusion. Any way you look at it, "The Enemy Within" is a STAR TREK classic. When THE NEXT GENERATION got around to trying its hand at a transporter duplicate story, seasoned hands produced a tale which is just as original in its own right as "The Enemy Within" was in 1966.

SECOND CHANCES

The writing staff for THE NEXT GENERATION has a term for scripts which involve duplicates of a regular character: "double trouble." Data, of course, has received the "double trouble" treatment in "Datalore," "Brothers," and, most recently, "Descent," which leads directly into the opening episode of the seventh season. Picard has been doubled twice, in the time-loop episode "Time Squared," and by an alien impostor in "Allegiance." Stories involving doubles are generally avoided, but, excepting the evil-twin cliché of "Datalore" (later transcended in "Brothers"), its rare occurrences have been handled well.

The sixth-season episode "Second Chances," which marked LeVar Burton's directorial debut, brought the "double trouble" scenario to bear on the character of Commander Will Riker. "Second Chances" was, first of all, definitely not an "evil-twin" episode. And it was not really a rehash of "The Enemy Within" by any stretch of the imagination. Instead, it proved to be a well-crafted episode which steered clear of any of the negative expectations aroused by its basic premise.

IDENTICAL BUT DIFFERENT

As "Second Chances" begins, the Enterprise is approaching a planet where, eight years earlier, Riker—then a lieutenant serving on the Potemkin— led the evacuation of a scientific expedition team threatened by seismic activity. The planet's powerful electromagnetic field interfered with transporters, and Riker, the last one off the planet, almost didn't make it. The Enterprise has come to retrieve the information left behind by the expedition, taking advantage of a periodic weakening of the EM field which will not reoccur for many years. When Riker beams down with an Away Team, tricorder readings reveal a survivor—who turns out to be another Riker, still clad in a tattered lieutenant's uniform!

It seems that when the Potemkin beamed up Riker, that ship's engineer used a second transporter beam to strengthen the one locked on to him. One beam brought Riker back to the ship while the other apparently bounced back off the EM field, beaming an identical Riker back to the surface. He has waited eight long years to be rescued. This is no good/evil problem: both Rikers have an equal claim to being the "real" Riker. And to further complicate matters, Lieutenant Riker never gave up his romantic feelings for Deanna Troi. He resumes his courtship of her and Deanna is confronted with reawakened feelings.

Commander Riker, on the other hand, takes an intense dislike to his alter ego. This gives Jonathan Frakes plenty of room for a great performance (or two). Lieutenant Riker is still ambitious and driven, ready to make up for lost time. Commander Riker is still ambitious but he's more at ease with himself. But Commander Riker, despite having reconciled himself to his friendship with Deanna, regrets that he gave up that and other things in his relentless ambition. It is this and other aspects of himself that really trigger his antipathy towards Lieutenant Riker.

ROOM FOR TWO

Lieutenant Riker's romantic pursuit of Deanna Troi actually succeeds, leading to further confusion. Commander Riker must readjust his thinking accordingly. Lieutenant Riker's presence on the Away Team led by the Commander leads to more friction. When a bridge collapses, one Riker must rescue the other, perhaps a nod to the solution of "The Enemy Within" but more likely a crisis which allows them to place their differences in perspective.

One daring idea came up while "Second Chances" was being scripted: the death of Commander Riker! This would have been a real zinger of an ending, a real shock to the show's occasional complacency that would still have left Jonathan Frakes with a job. But it would have wreaked havoc with the show's continuity. Every familiar situation would have made it necessary to explain everything to Lieutenant Riker, and so the idea was dropped.

Instead, Lieutenant Riker is assigned to the starship Gandhi. Riker sees him off, and gives him his trombone, on the feasible theory that half of everything Riker has owned longer than eight years belongs to his double. The Lieutenant decides to lessen the confusion by adopting his middle name, Thomas. And so another Riker is out there, living his own life.

"Second Chances" is one of the better NEXT GENERATION episodes of the sixth season, mining old ground but uncovering new treasures. The main difference between it and "The Enemy Within" is a simple one. Both Rikers are not different aspects of the same person, but are two fully developed individuals. The conflict between them arises as much from their similarities as it does from their differences. "The Enemy Within" is about meeting your evil aspect, and "Second Chances" is about meeting yourself and being forced to reconsider the choices you might have made differently. Each stands on its own strengths. Each is a product of its own time, and each is a worthy part of the STAR TREK mythos.

SHADES OF CHARACTER

In 1966, "The Corbomite Maneuver" established a concept which would be repeated a great deal throughout both the original STAR TREK, and THE NEXT GENERATION. Just because something is ugly doesn't necessarily mean that it's bad or evil. This would be extended into the philosophy that aliens have rights, too, even if they are non-human and impossible to understand by our standards.

This episode included one of those exchanges in which McCoy questions his captain's judgment. Kirk has promoted Dave Bailey to Lieutenant and McCoy thinks that he's putting too much pressure on the young man; expecting too much, too soon. Kirk and McCoy come close to blows over the issue, but Kirk restrains himself and later decides that perhaps McCoy was right.

During a tense sequence in "The Corbomite Maneuver" when an alien ship is threatening the Enterprise with destruction, Lt. Bailey cracks under the strain and starts screaming at the rest of the bridge crew that they've got to do something. Kirk has no choice but to confine Bailey to his quarters. Having characters react realistically to threats in a science fiction setting was something new.

The lighter side was dealt with realistically as well. When Kirk runs out of sickbay, complaining that McCoy didn't tell him there was an alert light flashing, McCoy remarks, while standing there alone, that if he jumped every time a light flashed around there he'd wind up talking to himself. A nice little bit, and appreciated.

Scripts which took the time to create believable characters helped STAR TREK to endure to the point that demands for a spin-off series were finally met. This meant that THE NEXT GENERATION had to try all the harder to work on the portrayals of the characters on the show. The fact of the matter is that in spite of how successfully Classic Trek handled characterization, subsequent science fiction series either overlooked or ignored this aspect of STAR TREK. Shows like SPACE 1999, FANTASTIC JOURNEY, LOGAN'S RUN, BUCK ROGERS, BATTLESTAR GALACTICA and others left no cliché unturned in its portrayal of wooden leading roles. It would just not do for THE NEXT GENERATION to stumble into that dead end as well.

ONE STEP FORWARD, TWO BACK

The Klingons were the black hat villains and evil standby's in the original STAR TREK. Roddenberry came to regret his simplistic approach to these characters and expanded their significance when he created THE NEXT GENERATION. This left a villainous void which needed to be filled.

Enter the Ferengi, the midget merchants of space. In "The Last Outpost," another old STAR TREK plot is swiped, this time from "Arena." A superior alien intelligence sees the Enterprise and another vessel bent on combat and renders both of them helpless. The alien wants to see what the personnel aboard the ship are really like and learn who the true aggressor is. Just as Kirk refused to see the Gorn destroyed when he triumphed, Riker turns down the offer to have the Ferengi ship destroyed after he triumphs. Cliché upon cliché.

In the more than one hundred episodes made since the Ferengi were introduced on TNG, they've returned several times, and each time they have been diminished in menace until they were reduced to annoyances at the bargaining table. In the sixth season episode "Rascals," when some Ferengi attempt to

WHOOPI GOLDBERG AND PATRICK STEWART ON JULY 18, 1991 AT THE PREMIERE OF SARAFI-NA.

© 1991
Ortega/Galell
a Ltd.

steal the Enterprise, the characters had been so diminished by then that it was difficult to take them seriously at all.

Due to their small stature and interchangeable personalities (they all talk, act and think alike), they became dull quickly. In fact in "Rascals," the Ferengi are defeated by children, which really hammered the nail in the myth of their menace. Early on it was said that even the Klingons feared the Ferengi, but that exaggeration has been quietly swept under the carpet. Saying something is scary and making it scary are clearly two different things.

SKELETON IN THE FAMILY CLOSET

The original STAR TREK introduced another villainous race in its first season that has managed to hang on and make a comeback in THE NEXT GENERATION.

"Balance Of Terror" presented the Romulans and their cloaking device, characters and technology which have been often reused in various versions of the show over the years. Basically this early STAR TREK episode is a retelling of the war movie THE ENEMY BELOW. The story even includes that submarine movie cliché wherein the commander discharges debris to make it appear that his ship has been destroyed. There's also the usual battle of nerves between the two commanders, as well as the need to "run silent" so that the enemy vessel won't detect their presence. In spite of these familiar elements, enough changes are wrung on the cliché to make it seem fresh and interesting, including a subplot involving racism.

Another subplot in "Balance Of Terror" involved a wedding which is interrupted permanently when the groom becomes the only casualty on the Enterprise during its clash with the Romulan ship. It brought a powerful human element into the conflict, showing that while the battle seemed to be between the two commanders, that other lives were at stake. STAR TREK learned early that genuine human touches could be just as pleasant and surprising as the larger triumphs in the storylines.

A PARADISE WITH TEETH

When Theodore Sturgeon wrote "Shore Leave," he came up with something quite different for the crew of the Enterprise to encounter. The episode is both a mystery and an adventure with elements which seem to smack too much of the fantastic to be real—which becomes the entire point. When Kirk and his crew embark on shore leave on a seemingly uninhabited world, they soon encounter people from their past as well as things which never existed. In the teaser, when McCoy encounters a white rabbit which proclaims, "Oh my paws and whiskers, I'll be late," and then a little girl following the rabbit's trail, we know that we're in store for something strange.

Kirk encounters two people he clearly has feelings for, only those feelings are direct opposites of each other. Ruth is an old lover he chooses to reunite with. Even after he learns the true nature of the world, he still wants to stay with her for awhile. But the one Kirk really gets involved with is an old adversary named Finnegan who had made his life a living hell when he was back in Starfleet Academy. It's largely a romp containing a single startling element of tragedy when Dr. McCoy is seemingly killed when he's impaled on the lance of a knight. McCoy was determined to prove that this was all an hallucination. He was wrong.

A significant note about "Shore Leave" is the basic premise of a place where anything you wish for can come true. In THE NEXT GENERATION that very notion has been refined and made a reality for crew members in the form of the holodeck. Although more control is exercised with the holodeck, it has been known to exhibit teeth as well, such as in "The Big Goodbye."

WHEN FANTASY BITES BACK

"The Big Goodbye" was the first of the big holodeck stories and it won a Peabody Award. This is a good story, although inexplicably TV GUIDE criticized it for being derivative of the Trek Classic episode "A Piece of the Action" just weeks before it garnered the Peabody Award for originality!

While the holodeck had been introduced in the premiere episode, this was the first time it was used as more than a background gimmick. This salute to hard-boiled detective fiction goes deeper than the superficial idea would at first suggest as it explores the concept that the holograms created by the holodeck might just have personalities and identities independent from their basic programming. This is hammered home when one of the Enterprise personnel suffers a real bullet wound and the other visitors to this "imaginary" setting are held captive.

When confronted with the reality of their existence, the holograms refuse to accept it, and two of them put it to the ultimate test and are destroyed, although the question is not addressed here as to what would happen if the deck recreated these characters. This is a story worthy of the best of Classic STAR TREK. Written by Tracy Torme, it is one of the top five episodes of this first season.

THE SUPPORTING ACTOR ALSO RISES

When Gene Roddenberry created STAR TREK in the '60s, he intended Kirk to be the lead and the others to be supporting performers. Spock emerged as a popular character even though he wasn't initially being played up on STAR TREK. Midway through season one, the rumblings of popularity had been heard.

It would be the second half of the first season before any episodes were done which spotlighted the Vulcan science officer and the first of these was "The Galileo 7," which first aired January 5, 1967. But unfortunately this episode did not showcase Spock as well as one might have hoped. Primarily it seemed to portray Spock's difficulty in dealing with non-Vulcans under stress. It also largely introduced what would become Spock's on-going friction with Dr. McCoy. But soon the Spock episode would air which the fans had been hoping for.

The dual nature of Mr. Spock was never better demonstrated than in Dorothy Fontana's wonderful script for "This Side of Paradise." In this story the Vulcan is exposed to spores which bring a person complete happiness and contentment. When the spores dominate Spock's body, they resolve all inner conflict. Since Spock's human nature was being repressed by his consciously followed Vulcan philosophy, the human side was freed. This is something which isn't always adequately made clear about Vulcans. They are not innately unemotional, it is a belief; almost like a religion. Showing emotion on Vulcan is considered to be in bad taste. It's a lifestyle, not a physiological state. This is why pon farr is considered such a private matter, because it is a throwback to when their race was ruled by its passions.

Essentially, "This Side of Paradise" introduced viewers to Leonard Nimoy. The late Jill Ireland as Leila is truly beautiful; even breathtaking. She and Nimoy compliment each other's performances marvelously and make a perfect couple. We actually come to enjoy seeing the two together on screen. In spite of the fact that, in a way, they have been brainwashed, we come to like this new and uncharacteristic Vulcan. The scene when Leila loses the spores and expresses regret is quite powerful. She doesn't regret being dominated by the spores because they allowed her to fulfill her long held desire to take Spock as a lover. It was some of the best drama seen on television in the 1966-67 TV season, but it was completely ignored by the Television Academy. After all, science fiction is just kid stuff, especially on television, or so they thought in the '60s. This prejudice remains active to this day.

THE EVIL TWIN SYNDROME

These days the concept of a lookalike for the hero has been reduced to the level of being a quickly recognized cliché known as the "evil twin." It's commonplace to see such descriptions for episodes in TV GUIDE. One can judge just how quickly a series is running out of creativity by how quickly they pull out the "evil twin" idea for an episode, as though we're not to supposed to notice how time-worn and old-hat the idea is. Virtually every low grade TV series of the past twenty years has done an "evil twin" story.

Sadly, THE NEXT GENERATION trotted out this hoary cliché awfully soon, which is one of many reasons why year one of NEXT GENERATION produced many episodes which are now unwatchable. When the coming attractions for "Datalore" actually referred to the character as "Data's evil twin," I laughed out loud, but unfortunately this episode is no joke. They actually took it seriously.

Lore is the android Dr. Soong created before Data, and he is thus Data's "brother." Lore has emotions but they are all negative, and he hates humans. There is even the obligatory scene where Lore impersonates Data and tries to make people think that Data is really Lore. The only good thing about this episode is that it returns to the planet where Data was found and reveals more about his origin.

The original writer's guide had Data having been created by aliens, but here it is revealed that an old scientist named "Noonian Soong" built him. Once again Roddenberry was forgetting his past as he'd already created a character on Trek Classic named "Khan Noonian Singh" who even returned in the big screen outing THE WRATH OF KHAN. But if you can't borrow from yourself, who can you borrow from? Thankfully, the subsequent writers and producers on THE NEXT GENERATION have only used Lore with great restraint, and then in stories which avoided all the evil twin clichés, almost as though they were embarrassed by how the character had been introduced.

AN ALIEN AMONG US

"Lonely Among Us" features a script by Trek Classic alumnus D.C. Fontana, based on a story by Michael Halperin. Unfortunately it again features ideas from the first series which are tripped over and stirred together in a warmed over brew. The Enterprise is transporting two feuding delegations of aliens (remember "Journey To Babel" in then second season of Classic Trek?) and it's all they can do to keep them apart, particularly when one faction is carnivorous and considers the other to be suitable prey.

But rather than exploring this further, the aliens remain portrayed in this superficial manner without any sort of resolution while the plot shifts to a disembodied alien entity which gets aboard when the ship passes through a strange cloud. The presence of the alien ambassadors primarily just serves as a juxtaposition to demonstrate the different kinds of aliens present in the universe. The one which accidentally gets aboard and finally takes over Picard's body, apologizes for all of the problems it caused while the guests aboard the Enterprise remain belligerent and uncooperative.

The mystery angle as the entity moves from one person to another is well handled and the fact that its intentions are not deliberately malevolent helps keep the story from sinking into cliché. Again this returns to Roddenberry's old favorite notion of what is different not necessarily being a threat. This idea goes back all the way to the '60s STAR TREK episode "The Corbomite Maneuver." This basic plot of an alien entity which steals aboard the Enterprise and then causes problems will become an old standby plot device as the series progresses. "The Bonding" and "Imaginary Friend" are two other NEXT GENERATION episodes using this plot device which come immediately to mind. While the idea is sometimes used in an imaginative fashion, it is nonetheless familiar.

An interesting side note is that a scene in the briefing room shows a model of the Galileo 7 in the background and it actually is the original special effects model of the shuttlecraft used in the sixties series.

ENTER THE MAN NAMED KHAN

The history of Earth in the 20th century was skirted as much as possible during the original STAR TREK series. The closest the '60s series came to dealing with this issue was in the episode "Space Seed."

When the Enterprise encounters a "sleeper ship" containing a crew in suspended animation, they discover that those aboard were launched into space in the 1990's. Thus they discuss the past Earth history of the 1990's, although it doesn't look as though we have to fear the Eugenics Wars taking place any time soon. But what "Space Seed" did do is make a specific reference to the Eugenics Wars as having taken place two hundred years before. That was the only solid information leading to the establishing of approximately when STAR TREK supposedly took place. But that has since been discarded as Classic Trek has been officially dubbed as taking place in the 23rd century with THE NEXT GENERATION being a 24th century adventure.

Ricardo Montalban was the perfect choice to play Khan. This episode establishes the character interplay between Kirk and Khan which formed such an important element of the 1982 motion picture sequel STAR TREK II—THE WRATH OF KHAN. In the minds of many fans, THE WRATH OF KHAN remains the best of the STAR TREK motion pictures. One unique aspect of Khan is that, aside from the generic villainy of the Romulans and the Klingons, Khan is one of the only overt villains to appear in the original 79 episode series. STAR TREK was never a villain-of-the-week show, but when THE NEXT GENERATION was hard pressed for script ideas, Roddenberry apparently decided that this might not be a bad direction to pursue.

RETURN OF A WARMED OVER IDEA

Just like "Encounter At Farpoint," the TNG episode "Hide And Q" (seen just a few weeks later) comes across as two stories which each work independently of the other. This was a common problem in many of the first season episodes of THE NEXT GENERATION. For instance, the opening part of the story in which the main characters find themselves battling foes assembled against them by Q has nothing to do with the last half of the story in which Riker accepts Q's gift of ultimate power, but must learn to use it wisely. Although supposedly from a superior culture, Q again comes across as just a playmate of Trelane (who romped through "Squire of Gothos" in Trek Classic).

Roddenberry seems to have forgotten much of what he did in the first STAR TREK series because the parallel with Trelane becomes even more pronounced when the climax of this episode is virtually identical to the resolution of "Squire of Gothos." In the '60s episode Trelane's parents come and drag him off. In "Hide And Q" other members of the Q race come and drag the bothersome entity away. Even John deLancie labels this as the worst of the Q episodes.

Riker is given tremendous powers by Q in "Hide And Q," but primarily only the obvious and the illogical happens as a result. The only good scene is when Riker had promised not to use his powers and as a result doesn't bring a child back to life, which he could have done. Riker accepts the consequences of keeping his word and his response to the situation on an emotional level is quite real. Too bad the series didn't have more writing in the first season such as that one sequence displayed.

AMAZONS AMONG US

In the '60s, television networks were uncomfortable with portrayals of strong female characters, otherwise the original STAR TREK would have played around with the old SF cliché of a society dominated by women. Roddenberry did explore the subject in the '70s TV movie PLANET EARTH and it was explored again in THE NEXT GENERATION in "Angel One," with only a few differences. While the men in this culture are portrayed as wimpy, the female ruling class are not Amazons by any means, which is one cliché avoided.

This story is rather thin as survivors of a star freighter accident have been living on that world for 7 years and have found women who prefer strong men. This has created an underclass who oppose the matriarchal society and want to exist separate from it, something those in charge find abhorrent and threatening. Finally the ruler demonstrates that she has compassion and spares the men and their wives from execution.

The script suffers from such painful use of 20th century anachronisms as "Bingo!" and "Will you still respect me in the morning?" Why someone would be paid for repeating clichés is beyond me. The real challenge for a writer is to avoid clichés and come up with interesting lines of dialogue which don't sound tired and familiar. "Angel One" is excruciatingly bad and reportedly even stopped filming during production in an effort to rewrite the story into something acceptable. They failed.

NOT BY THE NUMBERS

"11001001" by Maurice Hurley and Robert Lewin is a very good episode. It combines an interesting plot about the theft of the Enterprise with a further exploration of the advantages of the holodeck. This is a very fast paced story which has a great idea—get rid of everyone on the Enterprise so that Picard and Riker are the only characters left in the story from the regular cast. Stripped down to two, the story works very well and brings to mind some of the better episodes of Trek Classic.

This episode combines the often repeated "things aren't always what they seem" motif by revealing the intentions of the aliens to be strictly benevolent. A good added touch is that the aliens actually return to Starfleet to answer for their crimes. The relationship between Riker and the hologram, Minuet, is very interesting as there is real chemistry between the two and we feel Riker's sense of loss when she is gone from the computer banks along with the rest of the information the Binars had stored there.

Up until now the scripts on NEXT GENERATION seemed determined to give everyone equal time. But with the story stripped down to just Riker and Picard, these two finally emerge as the strong characters they are and show how much more interesting an episode is when they are the focus of the story. This episode clearly marked a turning point in the first season. Just as with the '60s STAR TREK, THE NEXT GENERATION was developing its own big three, consisting of Picard, Riker and Data. But unlike their '60s counterparts, wherein Kirk and Spock struggled for domination while McCoy existed in their orbit, Riker, Data and Picard have managed to attain a state of well managed equality.

SEARCHING FOR CHARACTERS

As the first year of the original STAR TREK drew to a close, all of the main characters were locked down and in place. Viewers knew the primary characteristics of Kirk, Spock and McCoy. Viewers even knew a few flourishes about Mr. Sulu and Nurse Chapel. Scotty was pretty much a cliché, but a likable one, and Uhura was the proud communications officer who said "Hailing frequencies open" better than anyone. But late in the first season of TNG, the search for who these people were was still going on. Riker, Data and Picard were coming more-or-less into focus, but the supporting cast seemed to be adrift. Some fine tuning was in order and they began with the most contro-versial cast member.

"Coming of Age" is an episode focusing on Wesley in which he doesn't save the Enterprise from destruction. The scenes with the Starfleet entry program are interesting although they beg the question of why people obviously this talented are winnowed down to just one candidate. The others are obviously possessed of their own remarkable skills as well. The scene in which Wesley undergoes his "psyche" test, in which he faces his deepest fear, is quite well done.

Written by Sandy Fries, this episode attempts to broaden Wesley's character once again in an effective story. The series is getting better at this point and this is a good episode with a strong emotional undertone which elevates it above typical TV science fiction fare. Roddenberry claimed to have rewritten the first dozen episodes of THE NEXT GENERATION, but it is only once we're past that largely unfortunate group that things start looking up.

Only "The Big Goodbye" emerges as a carefully written script in that first dozen and it is stylistically completely different from the other early episodes. "Coming of Age" was one of several Wesley episodes in the first season. Although Roddenberry very much liked this character, he had no counterpart in the '60s STAR TREK and no one connected with the series seemed to know what to do with him. They had no jumping off point as this was a child as a recurring character but Roddenberry had maintained that he would not do any "cute kid" stories. In television those tend to be the only kind of kid stories that TV writers know how to do.

THE WESLEY PROBLEM

The first season scripts which attempted to fine tune the character of Wesley came in response to what can only be described as a viewer backlash. Even fans who liked the first season of NEXT GENERATION tended to find Wesley a bit hard to take. In fact at a science fiction convention in Los Angeles in November 1987, a panel was held regarding the "Wesley Problem." Imagine everyone's surprise when Wil Wheaton showed up at the convention to defend his character.

Although the panel started out being much more critical of Wesley, even to including such suggestions as selling him to the Baron Harkonen (a particularly nasty character from the movie DUNE), panelists and audience members became more discreet when Wil Wheaton came up on stage. Panelists then explained that they had nothing against Wheaton as an actor but felt that Wesley was a particularly poorly written character.

Wheaton quickly became sensitive to criticism of Wesley Crusher in published interviews. In a STARLOG interview he proclaimed that he'd never save the Enterprise again and later claimed he'd actually only saved it twice. In 1988 when Roddenberry was questioned about storylines in which Wesley kept saving the ship, Gene tried to explain it by saying that it just so happened that a couple of scripts which did that happened to be filmed close together, which made it seem like a repeating theme.

Roddenberry seemed rather surprised by the criticism of Wesley, but the fact of the matter is that it was clear that the staff of THE NEXT GENERATION just didn't know how to write children at that time. As a result, Wesley's character was portrayed as being rather bizarre—neither a realistic child nor an adult, but something unsteadily in-between. In the second season the writers seemed to be trying to change this as Wesley became less of a cross between a genius and a foolish adolescent. By the time Wil Wheaton left the show at age 19, there was no way he could be written as a teenager any more as he was clearly a young adult. But he was seldom a very interesting character.

In the first season episode "Justice," when Wesley was threatened with execution, or in "Hide And Q" when he was shown being "killed," there was just nothing to connect with him on any level. He was just a kid and putting a child in jeopardy creates an automatic knee-jerk reaction, but that's about it. Wesley slowly matured, but his character never really deepened. In the fifth season episode "The First Duty," when Wesley was involved in a cover-up and only confessed after being confronted by Picard, it was one of the few times his character ever seemed truly human.

KLINGON GLORY

Originally Gene Roddenberry hadn't intended to include Klingons in THE NEXT GENERATION. But as NEXT

GENERATION went into production, Roddenberry changed his mind. Instead of ignoring the Klingons he would ennoble them.

In "Heart of Glory" we learn that not only wasn't Worf raised among Klingons, but he has rarely associated with them. This contrast is made especially strong when he's confronted by two of his race who hearken back to the warlike days when the Klingon Empire and the Federation were at odds back in the 23rd century. Had Worf encountered more diplomatic Klingons, the clash of wills would not have been so evident, if at all. But here his character is forced not only to deal with the difference between himself and these two members of his own race, but also with the vast cultural differences between himself and his fellow Enterprise crewmen.

Interesting touches abound in this story, such as the Klingon death chant which is chilling. The expressions on the faces of Worf's friends show their surprise and inner questioning better than any unnecessary dialogue could. The Klingon throwbacks, in spite of being more like the villains of Trek Classic, are also shown to have some dimension as well, such as when crewmen are arriving to arrest them and we think they are about to take a child hostage. The Klingons refuse to threaten the child because their sense of personal honor prevents them from warring on children.

Other Klingon episodes which have followed in subsequent seasons have each demonstrated how fascinating these characters can really be. The writing credits for this one go to Maurice Hurley for the script, based on a story by Maurice Hurley, Herb Wright and D.C. Fontana. Looking back over THE NEXT GENERATION, Worf's character is actually more precisely defined and explored in this episode than in any subsequent one. If anything as the series progressed it seemed to lose the focus it had achieved with Worf to the point that we understand him less now than we did in that excellent first season entry.

KEYING IN ON DATA

Although "We'll Always Have Paris" was apparently an attempt by THE NEXT GENERATION to give some more history to Picard by bringing back an old flame, another character overshadows Jean-Luc. Data emerges as the star in that episode. Just as Mr. Spock was given a healthy push by viewers of the original STAR TREK, Data was proving to be a goldmine of material for the staff writers on TNG. The plot involving experiments in non-linear time is so interesting that you don't need Picard's old girlfriend running around.

The time paradoxes are handled in a fascinating manner, particularly the scenes in which Data is sent in to do what only he could accomplish. This story spotlights Data in a far more interesting and dramatic fashion than anything in "Datalore" does. Some of these later first year episodes demonstrate more solid plotting and more complete exploration of the plot possibilities they present.

Sometimes in Trek Classic, an episode would also attempt to balance the scales equally between Kirk and Spock but end up with a story where Spock stole the show. This happened in "The Menagerie." That two-part episode was cobbled together using the first STAR TREK pilot starring Jeffrey Hunter as a flashback story inside new footage shot with Kirk and Spock. The fact that Spock was also in the original pilot enabled the two stories to have a logical continuity.

But in spite of Kirk having several vital scenes, it was Spock's story. Spock had served with Christopher Pike and now he was returning Captain Pike to the mysterious world of Talos IV. Even the climax of the episode turned into a character scene for Spock when Kirk accuses him of displaying flagrant emotionalism while Spock protests that he was completely logical about the entire affair.

Although Data has often been accused of being a Spock clone, the dynamics of his character are the opposite of Spock. Data is searching for the secret of human emotions and would actually be flattered were someone to suggest that he had any. Each character is meant to represent the contradictions of what it means to be human as one tries to turn away from it while the other seeks to embrace being human.

YES, BUT IS IT STAR TREK?

The most atypical STAR TREK episode of all time is THE NEXT GENERATION first year outing "Conspiracy."

Nothing in the STAR TREK canon is even remotely like this chilling tale of intrigue and horror. While Roddenberry had proclaimed that doing a show for syndication would remove many of the restrictions he operated under in the Classic Trek years, nothing had indicated that he was being anything but circumspect until "Conspiracy" aired. STAR TREK had never really tread on dangerous ground and throughout the first season THE NEXT GENERATION was equally inoffensive.

"Conspiracy" caught some fans by surprise because TNG had been playing it safe up until this point and had been seemingly going out of its way to avoid doing anything which anyone would find even remotely disturbing. The slow discovery of this plot begins as Picard is called to a secret meeting by an old friend, and it builds the suspense layer upon layer until we know that it is building up to one strange climax.

Employing state of the art makeup effects, a man controlled by the queen alien is eviscerated before our eyes in a scene which no doubt sent some light-hearted viewers screaming from the room because nothing like that had ever been seen on regular TV before. It upset some people, but so what? That's to be expected when you take risks. While at heart this is an old-fashioned alien invasion story, it has a tight plot, inner tension and a sense that the characters are actually involved in something life-threatening. This mood of impending destruction has only rarely been attempted since, though. Most notably this was again achieved in "The Best of Both Worlds" and "Yesterday's Enterprise."

PUSHING THE ENVELOPE

In May of 1988 when "Conspiracy" aired, fans were both delighted and repelled. Patricia Hayes of Sherman Oaks had a letter published in the L.A. TIMES which began, "I can't help but express my outrage with the 'Conspiracy' episode of STAR TREK—THE NEXT GENERATION that aired May 15. The story concerns an attempted takeover of the Federation and its higher-ups by alien life forms in the guise of oversized pink beetles. These creatures are seen entering and exiting the bodies of their victims by the mouth. The final 15 minutes of the program shows infected Federation officials dining on live worms, the graphic killing/dismemberment of an infected Starfleet officer and the mutated life form in the corpse's exposed innards.

"For the past seven months, STAR TREK—THE NEXT GENERATION has enjoyed a steady following (of which I am a part), high ratings and well-deserved praise for some truly fine stories. Now the show has shaken its credibility by delivering this inexplicable insult. I truly hope that executive producer Gene Roddenberry and the 'Conspiracy' authors are rebuked for their irresponsibility. It is bad enough that movies and the media in general are soaked with violence. To have this spill over into STAR TREK—THE NEXT GENERATION is inexcusable."

A REAL STORY FOR A CHANGE

A week later Jay Marks and Derik Vanderbeken replied in the letter column of the L.A. TIMES Calendar section. "Regarding Patricia Hayes' prudish letter criticizing the violence in the 'Conspiracy' episode of STAR TREK—THE NEXT GENERATION. Rather then an 'inexplicable insult,' 'Conspiracy' was far and away the best episode of the season. What a pleasure to see a show's writers tell a real story for a change, complete with drama, intensity, action (and yes, a little horror), rather than sit there and pat themselves on the back for their nobility and social consciousness.

"Instead of being 'rebuked for irresponsibility,' the show's production staff should be applauded for having the daring to finally produce an episode that takes full advantage of the fact that the show is syndicated and not subject to the ridiculously rigid restrictions of the network censors. After months of sitting through episodes that have been (with a few notable exceptions) pale rehashes of the original series or turgid little morality plays, timid enough for Saturday morning kidvid, we found it a sheer delight to see a little wicked fun. Here are two votes for more 'Conspiracy's,' less pabulum."

THE RETURN OF THE ROMULANS

Romulans were featured prominently in two of Classic Trek's most popular episodes: "Balance of Terror" and "The Enterprise Incident." Similar in many respects to the

Klingons of '60s STAR TREK, they were even portrayed as having an alliance with the Klingon Empire. The fact that "Balance of Terror" introduced them by having Mark Lenard play a Romulan with a conscience showed that they could conceivably be more than just typical villains. Instead, whenever antagonists were needed on Classic Trek, the Klingons got the nod and were always portrayed in the same simplistic manner.

Romulans figured in only two '60s episodes while stock footage of a Romulan warbird appeared in "The Deadly Years" as just a minor element. For all intents and purposes, the Romulans were all but ignored on the original STAR TREK. Their resurrection on THE NEXT GENERATION was long in coming and also suffered from a sense of not knowing what to do with them when they got there.

According to the episode "The Neutral Zone," the Romulans have not been heard from for fifty years—but that's not what the story is even really about! Three 20th century humans are found in suspended animation and the primary plot deals with their revival and their attempts to adjust to the 24th century. In shades of "Balance of Terror," there are also Federation outposts being mysteriously destroyed along the neutral zone frontier. Only this time it has nothing to do with the Romulans. It seemed like THE NEXT GENERATION version of a season cliffhanger and the abruptness at the end made it feel like it was the first part of a two-part story, only they forgot to say "continued next season" or "end of part one." As it turned out the elements introduced in this episode would only be followed up on in bits and pieces over the following two seasons. Then in "The Best of Both Worlds" at the end of season three we would finally understand what it all meant.

This season one finale, written by Maurice Hurley, from a story by Deborah McIntyr and Mona Clee, seems uneven because it introduces a mystery which is never specifically resolved. If the mysterious destruction of outposts in the Neutral Zone are the Borg (as we might conclude from a reference in season two's episode "Q Who"), then why are we led to believe later that the Borg were unaware of the Federation until Q brought the Enterprise into contact with them?

What "The Neutral Zone" actually does is re-introduce the Romulans to spice things up since the Ferengi proved to be a flop in the villain department. The Romulans at least have some dimension and in some ways can be used the way the Klingons were in Trek Classic, and their subsequent appearances in season two and beyond fill just that role.

THE CLIMAX OF YEAR ONE

The end of the first season of the original STAR TREK introduced one of its most memorable characters in "Devil In The Dark." This strange, blob-like mass known as the Horta, slithered into the hearts of viewers and created an indelible niche for itself. Few people recall that the Horta actually made its debut a couple of years earlier in an episode of THE OUTER LIMITS titled "The Probe." In both cases the creature was played by the late Janos Prochaska.

Prochaska, his son and others involved in a film project they were working on, were killed when their chartered plane crashed in the late '70s. Makeup artist Tom Burman (who later worked on STAR TREK III—THE SEARCH FOR SPOCK, among many other films) was working with Prochaska on the project as well, but missed going on that fatal flight due to an illness.

The first season of Classic Trek also produced the award-winning episode "City On The Edge Of Forever." It first aired April 6, 1967 and went on to take top honors at the World Science Fiction Convention for Best Dramatic Presentation of 1967. Harlan Ellison wrote it and it remains perhaps the single most popular STAR TREK episode ever presented. The original script Ellison wrote (before it was revised, unaccredited, by Gene Roddenberry) won the Writer's Guild Award for Best Dramatic Screenplay of 1967. Ellison's version of the script is available only in the 1976 anthology SIX SCIENCE FICTION PLAYS edited by Roger Elwood (which is out-of-print and not particularly easy to locate).

For two years plans have been in the works by Borderlands Press (the company owned by author Tom Monteleone) to reprint Ellison's original script along with special afterwards written by Leonard Nimoy and others. Ellison also plans to tell the entire story of his professional involvement with Gene Roddenberry for the first time, which will reveal facet's of Roddenberry's character never discussed publicly before. Ever since Roddenberry's death in October 1991, people have been more willing to come forward and reveal facts which had previously been kept private.

Many of these stories tend to shed light in facets of the STAR TREK years previously unacknowledged, such as William Shatner's recent contention that Gene Coon had as much to do with the success of the original STAR TREK as Roddenberry did. It would not be the first time that Roddenberry was accused of not wanting to give full credit to his collaborators.

THE CLASSIC—TNG CONNECTION

Gene Roddenberry was the one common factor in both of these STAR TREK series. But he also brought along Dorothy Fontana and David Gerrold to assist in the shaping and development of THE NEXT GENERATION. Dorothy Fontana was a script writer and story editor on the '60s STAR TREK and Gerrold wrote the popular second year episode "The Trouble With Tribbles," as well as contributing to "I, Mudd" and "The Cloud Minders." Both Gerrold and Fontana had retained a high profile connection with STAR TREK over the years.

On THE NEXT GENERATION, Gerrold reportedly contributed a lot of ideas for Data as well as Geordi LaForge. He also wrote one script, a parable about AIDS, which was never produced. Fontana also contributed heavily to the development of TNG as well as working on several first season teleplays. But behind-the-scenes disagreements led to a falling out among them. Gerrold and Fontana ultimately filed grievances with the Writer's Guild against Roddenberry, and Paramount settled with them behind-the-scenes. In spite of it all, Roddenberry managed to retain sole screen credit for the creation of STAR TREK— THE NEXT GENERATION.

Unlike season one of the original STAR TREK, which produced some of its finest episodes, THE NEXT GENERATION got off to a rocky start, so rocky that looking back it's a wonder there was ever a season two. While Trek Classic had its occasional low points in its first season, such as "The Alternative Factor," TNG often seemed clueless as to what they were trying to accomplish. Picard began as a cranky starship captain who

WIL
WHEATON
OF THE
NEXT GEN-
ERATION.

apparently disliked children while Beverly Crusher seemed to still have some misgivings about serving under a captain who had sent her husband to his death. But both of these subplots were quickly abandoned, just as brief references to a past relationship between Riker and Troi were ignored for several years.

WOMEN ON THE ENTERPRISE

Female characters on STAR TREK, both in the '60s and in the modern version, have suffered from careless handling. Uhura may have been presented as a equal, but she was never given an equal say nor an equal part of the plot action—ever. Nurse Chapel had one episode which brought her character to the foreground, "What Are Little Girls Made Of?", and then she was relegated to being little more than a gofer.

On NEXT GENERATION, Troi spent whole seasons just taking up space while contributing little. It was only after Roddenberry's involvement with TNG was greatly reduced that Troi's character was explored beyond the relationship with her clownish mother, Lwaxana (played by Majel Barrett Roddenberry). Only in seasons five and six has Troi been allowed to develop much of any character.

Beverly Crusher's character received even worse treatment than Uhura and Chapel. Fired from THE NEXT GENERATION after the first season because she "didn't fit in" with the other characters, she was rehired in season three after her replacement, Diana Muldaur, was perceived as being even less successful in fitting in with the other regular characters. Again, not until seasons five and six of TNG was Dr. Crusher given any scripts which focused on her character and allowed her to truly come to the fore. Her absence in season two was never referred to and when she was brought back in season three there's only a couple perfunctory scenes in which she and Wesley discuss her previous absence.

In the world of STAR TREK, whether in the 23rd century or the 24th century, men seem to be in charge while women are "allowed" to achieve some occasional measure of success. But then is was during the enlightened '60s, with STAR TREK's multi-racial and sexually integrated crew that the women all wore mini-skirts while costumes for other female characters were designed to be as provocative as possible. Even Roddenberry said he liked viewers to see women on the show wearing costumes which seemed like they might fall off at any moment.

THE SECOND SEASONS

Spock had already emerged as one of the most popular elements of STAR TREK and so it was only logical that year two of Classic Trek would lead off with a story which delved into the Vulcan's background. "Amok Time," written by Theodore Sturgeon, premiered on September 15, 1967 and revealed that Vulcans have a sex drive, whether they want it or not. Pon Farr is, basically, comparable to when an animal goes into "heat," and in this case the Vulcan needs a wife in order to complete the mating ritual.

THE NEXT GENERATION didn't start entirely fresh with year two. The premiere episode, "The Child," was reworked from a script for the proposed but never accomplished STAR TREK II television series which Paramount had been seriously planning back in 1978! That series would have featured most of the original cast, with the exception of Spock. Xon, a different Vulcan, would have been on the bridge in Spock's place in order to make things seem more like STAR TREK had always been. In order to be retailored for THE NEXT GENERATION, the script had to be completely rewritten to incorporate the new cast. It still turned out to be a weak, if manipulative, entry.

While "The Child" did feature Deanna Troi more prominently, she was portrayed as treating her alien offspring as though he were a normal, human child. Instead of Troi trying to get to know the alien better and understand what he's all about, she continually relates to him based on his superficial resemblance to a human being. She says she can't help the way she feels. The script just pointed up the inability of the writers to script female characters in any manner outside limited confines of emotional stereotypes.

In "Amok Time" we meet Spock's betrothed, T'Pring, whose existence comes as quite a surprise to Christine Chapel. T'Pring is Vulcan through and through and comes across as a much stronger female character than virtually any other ever seen on STAR TREK. She's made her decisions and decided that no matter what happens at the ceremony, she wins. She's the only woman ever seen on STAR TREK who looks as though she could cause her Vulcan husband to become henpecked. When Spock releases her from her vow, he actually looks relieved!

This is also the famous episode where Spock chases Chapel out of his quarters and shouts at his captain as he demands shore leave on Vulcan. Perhaps it's a residual effect of the pon farr which results in Spock's later emotional reaction when he discovers that his captain is still alive at the end of the story.

LET'S DO IT AGAIN

"Amok Time" had whole sections of its action and story structure pilfered by THE NEXT GENERATION in its first season episode "Code of Honor." Written by Kathryn Powers and Michael Baron, it has structural elements from "Amok Time" in both the climactic fight and its resolution. Since Roddenberry proclaimed to all who would listen that he rewrote the first dozen episodes of TNG, this could arguably be blamed on STAR TREK's creator who would borrow from himself and assume that no one would notice.

"Code of Honor" quickly goes downhill. An all black culture is an interesting idea, particularly the matriarchal angle (which would be repeated in "Angel One"), but most of that is pushed into the background in order to stage a fight which has obvious parallels with "Amok Time" in the resolution (the one who apparently dies is revived aboard the Enterprise).

Picard makes a lot of angry noise in this episode over the kidnapping of his Security Chief, but in the end seems impotent to really accomplish anything. Why he must follow their bizarre protocol while they can flagrantly violate the Federation's at will without reprisal is stretched much too far. Picard should have stressed Federation protocol just as strongly as the Ligonians did theirs, and then backed it up. The Ligonians enjoy too much challenging a stronger foe and then watching him cower. This is not a fine portrayal of a strong starship captain. Picard comes across as being woefully inexperienced and far outclassed by the comparatively primitive Ligonians.

Once again there seems no consistency in the characterization of the new Enterprise captain, particularly since it had already been established that his previous starship command lasted 22 years! Where is the savvy and the experience in dealing with alien societies? All in all the story plays like a first draft script in need of several rewrites.

The character of Jean-Luc Picard had clearly not been very well thought out when THE NEXT GENERATION began filming. Within half a dozen episodes of the original STAR TREK, we knew where Jim Kirk was coming from, where he was going and pretty much what he would do in any given situation. Instead of defining his character and sticking to it, Picard was all too often portrayed as a whining bureaucrat who let himself get pushed around. Then when Picard did turn around and hit back in some manner, it was completely unexpected and made one wonder why he seemed so spineless on other occasions.

Patrick Stewart was reportedly so unhappy with the scripts during the first year of THE NEXT GENERATION that he was constantly fighting with the producers. The other actors weren't any happier with them and often stood behind Stewart in his complaints.

LIFE ABOARD

The concept of a parallel universe where the familiar is given a twist to produce something tinged with darkness can produce exciting results in the right hands. Classic Trek did their version of an alternate universe Enterprise in its second season while THE NEXT GENERATION went in a completely different direction with that notion in season three.

Written by Jerome Bixby, the second season Classic Trek episode "Mirror, Mirror" dealt with the parallel universe concept and handled it perfectly. In the alternate reality, the Enterprise crew are essentially Klingons in thought, act and deed. I've always wondered what it would have been like if Kirk had met some Klingons in the alternate universe and had to team up with them against the Enterprise. This episode cried out for a sequel, but unfortunately one was never done.

But THE NEXT GENERATION presented the stunner of them all in this regard. "Yesterday's Enterprise" is an alternate universe/time travel story that's the equal of the best shows done on Trek Classic. When the Enterprise 1701-C, the version from 20 years before, appears in this timeline, history is changed and we suddenly find a darker, grimmer Enterprise with Picard in command, fighting a continuing war with the Klingons. Denise Crosby returns as Tasha Yar, who comes to realize that she isn't supposed to be there, or even be alive. Her sacrifice to help put time right again is a far more fitting send-off than her off-hand death back in the first season's "Skin Of Evil."

The alternate universe aspect is handled meticulously and the complicated science fiction aspects of the storyline are presented without stopping to present a blackboard explanation with diagrams. This is science fiction equal with the complexity of some of the better prose science fiction published today, and the script bears the names of six writers required to pull it off! This show has drama, action and the kind of details which make any story memorable. This third year TNG episode showed that the staff was finally getting people who knew how to script realistic female characters, but for Tasha Yar it was too little, too late.

AN OLD IDEA

"The Deadly Years" afflicts Kirk and his main officers with a deadly disease causing accelerated aging. Spock ages the slowest thanks to the longevity of Vulcans, but McCoy's efforts to find a cure are hampered by his own senescence. A Commodore on board convenes a hearing and removes the now nearly-senile Kirk from command.

This rated as one of DeForest Kelley's favorite episodes. As his character aged, Kelley had him become more and more the old-fashioned country doctor McCoy really envisioned himself as. "Yes, I began to fall back. I had that in mind from the beginning, that the older he became, the more he would fall back into what he really had a feeling in his heart for. Fortunately, it worked very well. There was a great disturbance at the studio at the time because they felt I should have been nominated for that show, but I was not. They were very upset about it." Nimoy, however, would again receive an Emmy nomination for the second season, although he didn't win.

THE NEXT GENERATION dipped back into "The Deadly Years" when it produced "Unnatural Selection," a quick reworking of the story with an ending lifting directly from another "Deadly Years" take-off done in the animated STAR TREK series. Less than satisfying. The episode is the only one which features Dr. Pulaski as a major character as opposed to a minor character. It may have been about this time that Roddenberry started rethinking his decision to replace Dr. Crusher.

Pulaski was basically portrayed as a female Dr. McCoy. Just as Spock and McCoy had a friendly rivalry, an attempt was made to create some sort of spirited interplay between Pulaski and Data, but it was only a half-hearted attempt and was dropped after a few episodes. Pulaski was portrayed as being irascible without being particularly interesting.

KLINGONS ARE PEOPLE, TOO

Whenever Classic Trek needed a villain, the Klingons always seemed to be handy. In the second season of the '60s series, the Klingons turned up making trouble in "Friday's Child," "The Trouble With Tribbles" and "A Private Little War." The Klingons were always portrayed as untrustworthy back-stabbers with nothing to recommend them. They were just simplistically set up to portray stock villains. They were like the Germans in movies made during World War Two.

On THE NEXT GENERATION, Gene Roddenberry changed everything about the Klingons. Their villainous days were all in the past and they actually had a culture far more interesting and complex than anything the '60s STAR TREK might ever have hinted at. In fact, TNG not only had a Klingon serving on the Enterprise, but its second season featured an episode in which Riker temporarily transferred to a Klingon vessel to serve as its first officer.

"A Matter Of Honor" is far and away the best episode in the second season of THE NEXT GENERATION. When Riker is transferred to a Klingon ship as part of an exchange program, personality clashes abound along with vivid portrayals of life aboard a Klingon ship. It's superb. This is the second of THE NEXT GENERATION's Klingon episodes, many of which are top of the line material. "A Matter of Honor" demonstrates what is lost by having everyone aboard the Enterprise so unrealistically gracious to each other all the time; it's called conflict.

Some of the best moments in the original STAR TREK occur when Kirk and McCoy disagree and get angry, and when McCoy has his fill of Spock's Vulcan approach to everything. That's the way real people act! Real people get angry! They act irrational! In "The Menagerie" McCoy mentions how he or Kirk might run off half-cocked if they thought they had a good reason, but not Spock. Not a Vulcan.

ALL THAT FUNNY STUFF

It was during the original STAR TREK's second season that they began doing humorous episodes such as "The Trouble With Tribbles." "Tribbles" makes no pretense at being serious at any time. Stanley Adams as Cyrano Jones is clearly meant to be Harry Mudd, but Roger C. Carmel apparently wasn't available for filming at that time. Mudd did reappear later in the second season, though, in "I, Mudd," which was an out and out farce.

Just a couple weeks later another humorous episode, "A Piece Of The Action," premiered and pitted the Enterprise crew against gangsters in the mold of Al Capone and old Chicago on an alien world. Everything conveniently looked just like 20th century Earth, making costuming and location shooting easier than most. The episode actually would have been more amusing had the aliens mixed up the gangland trappings of 20th century Earth with alien ideals of their own. Instead it comes across as a cheaply made episode, filmed on the backlot using costumes from central casting. It remains a well-liked story, though.

The imitative nature of the people on the planet Iotia formed the germ of an idea which David Gerrold wanted to follow up on in THE NEXT GENERATION. He wanted to have the Enterprise-D return to that world and discover that the people had been so enamored of Kirk and Spock that they elevated them to godhood with statues and the like. Gerrold saw it as a great way to do a parody of STAR TREK fandom. At the time, Roddenberry didn't want any sort of crossovers with the old series, and when Gerrold and Roddenberry had a bitter falling out some months later, it precluded the story idea ever being done.

While THE NEXT GENERATION has had humorous subplots now and then, they've never really gone all out and done anything like "A Piece of the Action" or "I, Mudd." Perhaps the producers of TNG couldn't quite get next to the idea of seeing the crew of the Enterprise engaging in slapstick comedy. Or perhaps the episode in which Data conjured up Joe Piscopo on the holodeck to teach him about comedy cured them of any ambitions in that direction.

FAMILY REUNIONS

The second seasons of both Classic Trek and THE NEXT GENERATION had episodes in which major characters reconciled with their estranged fathers.

"Journey to Babel" finally introduces Spock's parents. The occasion is a diplomatic mission. A ship is following the Enterprise; the Tellerite ambassador is murdered and Sarek is the prime suspect. Sarek needs a blood transfusion for a heart operation but Spock must act as captain after an Andorian stabs Kirk. Kirk fakes his recovery so Spock can give blood. A battle with the ship results in its destruction. Kirk's attacker kills himself after revealing that he killed the Tellerite ambassador, and Spock and his father achieve a rapprochement after nearly twenty years of estrangement.

In spite of the subplot involving Spock and his parents, the drama is actually soft-peddled. In fact the scene near the end when Spock and Sarek are both in sickbay is played for laughs as McCoy uses his position as their physician to make them be quiet, and thereby getting in the last word.

"The Icarus Factor" deals with Riker having a showdown with his father while Worf undergoes a painful ritual in the holodeck. In Riker's case he has to contend with his overly competitive father. The script tries very hard but the stories don't quite gel. What emerges most strongly is Riker's reconciliation with his father, Kyle, as they bury the hatchet over old complaints.

Meeting Riker's father makes it clear where Will Riker gets his stubborn streak. That character trait of Will's is one that we've seen emerging gradually over the two seasons, particularly when Lt. Riker displays his temper. The fact that we even know he has one is a sign that the characters are beginning to have some genuine humanity to them.

NEW VILLAINS, OLD VILLAINS

While special effects were never a vital element of STAR TREK. However, some stories did require a more than average use of them. "The Doomsday Machine," written by Norman Spinrad, not only was a special effects showcase but gave special guest star William Windom a script he could sink his teeth into. Windom was Commander Decker of the Constellation, and he blamed himself for the death of his entire crew. That crew met their end after the spaceship was attacked by a gigantic weapon and the crew escaped by beaming down to a nearby planet. What they hadn't realized was that this weapon specialized in pulverizing and destroying entire worlds, which it promptly proceeded to do.

No origin for the robot weapon called The Doomsday Machine was ever revealed. But could it be that hints of where it came from may finally be coming to light in THE NEXT GENERATION with the introduction of the Borg?

A key episode in the entire STAR TREK series is "Q Who," which introduces the Borg and sets up the confrontation which won't take place until over a year later. It's also the first decent episode with Q. Although it's made clear in the conclusion that because of this encounter the Borg will now come in search of the Federation, early in the episode a reference is made to the destruction of outposts in the TNG episode "The Neutral Zone" from the previous year.

That would indicate that a Borg scout ship had previously been in Federation space even before Q forced the confrontation between the Enterprise and the Borg. The presence of Q leads to the death of eighteen crew members when the Borg slice out a section of the Enterprise for examination. While the special effects in Trek Classic were much better than some people make them out to be, they never did anything close to what is seen in this episode.

THE NATURE OF HUMANITY

On the original STAR TREK, Spock did his utmost to be the perfect Vulcan by denying his humanity. On THE NEXT GENERATION, the android Data tried to deny his artificial nature by proving that he could be just as human as the next man.

"The Measure Of A Man" is another well-written entry as the matter of Data's humanity is explored in depth from a legal standpoint. When an aggressive and overbearing Federation officer wants to disassemble Data to find out what makes him so unique, Picard argues against it in a stirring episode.

"Pen Pals" is a touching episode in which the Prime Directive is invoked when Data want's to save an alien child whose distress call he's received. The problem is that this planet is at a primitive stage in which contact with off world societies would interfere with the planet's normal cultural development. The way Data deals with the problem honestly and effectively demonstrates that he has more humanity than we're often led to believe.

THE SECOND SEASON CLIMAX

"Contagion" is a fine TNG episode in which the Romulans return after the Enterprise unsuccessfully attempts to aid a sister ship, the Yamato, in the neutral zone. The destruction of the Yamato is startling and the race by the crew of the Enterprise to prevent the same thing happening to them is well wrought. The uneasy truce with the Romulans is very well portrayed here and this episode begins to establish the Romulans as the kind of on-going adversary that the Klingons were in Trek Classic. But while the Romulans are portrayed as antagonists, they are also given more dimension than the old version of the Klingons were.

"The Emissary" is another Klingon episode with a twist. A ship with Klingons in suspended animation from the bad old days defrosts and then goes after the Enterprise. It's a fine Worf episode which introduces his old flame, K'Ehleyr, a character who will be needlessly killed off in season three. Worf's old lover, played by Suzie Plakson, brings out sides of Worf not seen before. He clearly still has feelings for her and is even willing to honor her in the proper Klingon fashion. But in this case she is the one placing herself outside normal Klingon society as she rejects Worf's traditional beliefs.

Just when we meet another Klingon character who's as interesting as Worf, the writers chose to kill her off in her next appearance.

PATHS NOT TAKEN

"Assignment Earth" was the final episode of the second season of Classic Trek. At the time it was shown it came across quite well even though it was the pilot for another proposed series and the Enterprise crew really only had second billing in it. Robert Lansing as Gary Seven was a human taken from Earth years before and raised on another planet by aliens who are interested in overseeing Earth's destiny to prevent the planet's self-destruction.

The story, set in 1968 when Earth was (supposedly) launching orbiting nuclear bombs, is clearly dated but still plays well. In a supporting role as Roberta Lincoln is a young actress named Terri Garr, who years later would make her mark in such feature films as YOUNG FRANKENSTEIN and CLOSE ENCOUNTERS OF THE THIRD KIND.

The episode has some nice new gimmicks, such as the weapons pen carried by Gary Seven, his black cat Isis and a computer which can teleport him in a manner different from the transporter the Enterprise uses. In fact the Enterprise first encounters Gary Seven when they accidentally intercept his transporter beam and suspect him of being a hostile alien surgically altered to pass for human.

Basically the story has Kirk and Spock tracking down Gary Seven while he strives to heroically complete his mission. If there are any villains in the piece, it's the United States for launching a nuclear satellite to begin with.

"Assignment: Earth" would have been the first official STAR TREK spin-off, but unlike THE NEXT GENERATION it would have been set in the 20th century. Since STAR TREK wasn't a ratings success in the '60s, there was no call at the time for a slightly different version of the Enterprise and its crew. That would have to wait for two decades before the time was ripe.

THE THIRD SEASONS

The survival of STAR TREK into its third season is the stuff of legends. When indications were revealed that NBC was considering canceling the show, a letter writing campaign was organized by Bjo Trimble. The write-in campaign was so successful that NBC received over a million letters urging that the series be spared, although the network would only admit to receiving about two hundred thousand letters.

THE NEXT GENERATION needed no such show of special support. By the time its third season rolled around the series was more popular than ever. But that didn't mean that everything was running smoothly. They had decided that a small miscalculation had been made.

Year three saw the return of Gates McFadden as Dr. Beverly Crusher. She had been let go (fired?) at the end of the first year and replaced by Diana Muldaur. There was the usual sturm und drang from the fans when she was replaced, and even a letter-writing campaign ensued, but Gene Roddenberry stated publicly that it was his decision and he wouldn't change his mind.

But by the end of year two he had changed his mind. It was decided that although Muldaur was a good actress, her chemistry with the other performers wasn't what they were looking for, and that in fact Gates McFadden had worked out better after all. She returned in season three with the same lack of ceremony with which Diana Muldaur had both joined and left the show.

THE RODDENBERRY TOUCH

How important was Gene Roddenberry's presence on the original STAR TREK? Fred Freiberger was brought in by the network to replace Roddenberry as the line producer when Gene quit over the network's reneging on its promise to give STAR TREK a prime Monday night time slot. NBC hired Freiberger and he proceeded to alienate many people connected with the series.

Season three of Classic Trek got off to a less than auspicious start with a real howler called "Spock's Brain." The less said about it the better as it's just a boring story about scantily clad Amazons who beam aboard the Enterprise, knock everyone out, scoop the Vulcan's brain out of his body and race back to their homeworld to use Spock's brain to run their master computer. When they manage to trace the Amazons to their planet, they discover the computer which speaks to them in Spock's voice! Think about it.

By the time of the third season of THE NEXT GENERATION, Gene Roddenberry had largely turned over the production to Rick Berman and others. The producers and the writing staff had a handle on the characters and they knew what style of television series they were creating. The show held its own in the third season, with as many good episodes as season two had, while also producing the single most outstanding episode of the first three years. In these respects THE NEXT GENERATION was nothing like Trek Classic as the original series had a strong second season which was not quite as good overall as season one, and a miserable third season. So comparisons along those lines are non-existent. If anything they run in opposite directions. While the '60s STAR TREK was clearly winding down in its third season, NEXT GENERATION was still winding up.

A VERY UNUSUAL ALIEN

Season three of TNG opened on an only average note with "Evolution," a story about a scientist obsessed with getting the Enterprise to a location where he can perform a once-in-a-lifetime experiment. This becomes complicated when one of Wesley's experiments, involving nanites (microscopic robots) gets out of control and threatens the ship. It's an average episode and hardly the stuff of a good season-opener.

"Ensigns Of Command" is a much better TNG episode and more worthy of the lead slot in a season. It deals directly with the concept of having to compromise and accept the inevitable. Relations with an alien race require that the Federation evacuate the human colonists on a planet. But the colonists refuse to cooperate and insist that they will stand and fight for their colony. In a display of brutal honesty over negotiation, Data demonstrates the futility of their resolve by using his phaser to destroy part of the colony, demonstrating exactly what they would be up against. In the face of such overwhelming odds, the colonists are forced to capitulate. An excellent episode. In this episode Data seems very Spock-like as he challenges the position the colonists take and finally just coldly demonstrates how wrong they are.

"The Survivors" is another top-notch entry, and continues the attempts by the series to come up with ideas never explored by STAR TREK before. When the Enterprise discovers two human survivors on a planet devastated by an alien attack, their curiosity is only heightened by the fact that the modest dwelling occupied by these two old folks is the only patch of ground on the planet not obliterated. The couple refuses to be evacuated and finally the man reveals that he is a being of a species previously unknown to the Federation.

The alien had taken human form to marry a human woman he'd fallen in love with, but even though he has massive powers, his kind are strictly pacifists. His wife chose to join the colonists in trying to fight the alien attackers, and when she died along with the others, the man struck out in his grief, destroying not only the attacking ship, but every last member of the race the ship represented, throughout the universe!

Even though NEXT GENERATION is a spin-off of the original STAR TREK, the structure of the scripts and type of shows done are very different. But "The Survivors," in spite of being an excellent story, is very simply told. The Enterprise arrives at a planet and encounters a mystery. On a very basic level it follows the mold of the '60s STAR TREK and by plugging in the old Enterprise crew to replace the new one, "The Survivors" could easily have been a Classic Trek episode. Even the underlying concept of a pacifist resorting to violence and feeling profound regret and recriminations is very much in the Roddenberry mold.

THE UPSIDE DOWN ENTERPRISE

The third year of Trek Classic was so wild and inconsistent that it is virtually impossible to draw parallels between it and what was done years later on THE NEXT GENERATION. Themes and storylines explored on STAR TREK during its third season in the '60s seldom achieved parity or continuity with what had gone before. The Klingons did return in one episode, "Day of the Dove," and the Romulans turned up in "The Enterprise Incident," an episode which has an equal number of fans and detractors.

"The Tholian Web" was another special effects highlight of the series with a better than average script. The special effects were so outstanding that this episode was nominated for an Emmy in that category, and received a special "close-up" in that week's TV GUIDE featuring a photo of the Enterprise—printed upside down. Amazingly, the story is well handled from beginning to end. It's basically a Spock/McCoy episode as Captain Kirk vanishes in act one and isn't rescued from limbo until act four. In the mean time McCoy questions Spock's command decisions even more brutally than he ever did Captain Kirk's. Finally though McCoy and Spock settle their differences over a ceremony in which they acknowledge that Kirk must be dead and play his final instructions for them, which puts all of their personal differences in perspective.

The third season of the '60s STAR TREK stressed drama more than ever, and with the pre-existing friendly rivalry between Spock and McCoy, that was just played up to its utmost, even to having McCoy confront Spock on the bridge in one scene, grab the center seat and spin it around to face him as though McCoy was about to take the Vulcan on man-to-man. With Spock commanding the Enterprise while Kirk is lost in space, McCoy is called upon to whip up yet another of his miracle cures, just as he did in "Miri" and in "The Naked Time."

ADVERSARIAL ALIENS

"The Enterprise Incident" is both a good and a bad Classic Trek episode. The part of the storyline of Kirk being altered to look Romulan is well handled. In this way Kirk can sneak aboard a spacecraft to steal a Romulan cloaking device. But otherwise the script has some real problems. The unemotional Mr. Spock becomes emotionally involved with a female Romulan commander. The script by D.C. Fontana was rewritten against her wishes and she has always complained about this. Fred Freiberger, years later in an interview, claimed she was out of town when he needed a rewrite, a fact Fontana denies. Still, the Romulan commander from this episode has remained a popular character among Trek Classic fans. This may well be because she remains one of the only two romantic entanglements Spock had during the entire STAR TREK series. The other one was Leila Kalomi in "This Side of Paradise" and Spock was not being himself in that episode.

The Romulans were an interesting and underused contingent in the original STAR TREK universe. "The Enterprise Incident" is literally only the second episode in which Romulans figured prominently and the second year of Classic Trek skipped them entirely except as an appearance via stock footage at the end of "The Deadly Years." The Romulans have a fascinating history, both with an ancestry linked to Vulcan and a past war fought with the Federation. But the possibilities inherent in these characters remained largely unexplored on the original STAR TREK.

THE NEXT GENERATION decided to remedy that. "The Enemy" is a follow-up to last season's "Contagion" as the Romulans are back in the position the Klingons occupied in Trek Classic. When a crashed Romulan scout ship attracts the attention of the Enterprise, a Romulan warship soon appears in an attempt to cover up an obvious spy mission. But when Geordi becomes lost on the planet with a Romulan survivor he's found, the two are forced to help each other to survive. But the opposite happens aboard the Enterprise. When a wounded Romulan needs a blood transfusion from Worf in order to survive, the Klingon refuses because his real parents were killed by Romulans when he was just a child. Worf's character has never been more forceful and compelling than he is in this story.

The Ferengi are back in "The Price," but the fact that they are portrayed as buffoons shows the rethinking that went into them after it was realized that four foot tall, wise-cracking aliens do not make for menacing opponents. The arrogance of the Ferengi is what makes them funny, particularly in the scene when they refer to Worf as Picard's Klingon servant. It's a wonder Worf didn't kill them when that remark was made.

WELL CRAFTED WRITING

The third season of Classic STAR TREK is notorious even among people who know little about the show. If someone who has only a passing interest in STAR TREK watches an old episode and doesn't like it, they'll ask, "Is this a third season episode? I hear those were pretty bad." With that twenty year shadow hanging over them, the staff of THE NEXT GENERATION seemed to push themselves to the limit to insure that such a third season rap would never be attached to them.

Beginning with "The Survivors," THE NEXT GENERATION started doing more location shooting and it added immeasurably to the realism of the planet exteriors. Dark, turbulent worlds can be pulled off on a sound stage, but Class M (earth-like) planets look like sound stages when they're shot indoors.

"Who's Watching The Watchers" deals with the Prime Directive and how it is inadvertently violated when a primitive people observe some Federation scientists who'd been observing them. When they see Enterprise crewmen beam in, they assume that they are being visited by gods. It's up to Picard to try to undo the mess and keep the planet from wallowing in superstition and thereby harming its natural development. A provocative theme dealt with intelligently. This episode was a personal favorite of Gene Roddenberry's.

"The Bonding," written by Ronald Moore, is an emotionally wrenching story which returns to the fact that the Enterprise crew have their families with them, a facet all but ignored throughout the second season. When a little boy's mother dies while exploring an ancient world with an Away Team, Worf feels responsible because he was in charge of the detail.

Wil Wheaton is given a rare opportunity to do some genuine acting when he's called upon to talk with the boy because of his own loss of a parent he suffered when he was that boy's age. Wes Crusher resists the position this puts him in until the climax. By that time everyone involved is confronting their inner turmoil and facing that which cannot be avoided, accepting death and the grief that comes with it.

Coincidentally, "The Bonding" follows close on the heels of "The Survivors," another story which deals with death and grief, subjects rarely tackled in science fiction television which all too often gets wrapped up in exploring ideas more than feelings. But then STAR TREK has always tried to do both whenever possible.

THE MANY FACES OF WAR

The Romulans again return in "The Defector," which turns out to be a direct sequel to "The Enemy." The Enterprise picks up a Romulan defector who turns out to be an admiral determined to head off a war between his people and the Federation. He reveals plans for a sneak attack slated to be launched from the Neutral Zone, but he turns out to be a plant.

While his reason for defecting is real, the Romulans had manipulated him so that they could lure a Federation starship inside the Neutral Zone and capture it. The surprise which Picard has up his sleeve in anticipation of such a trap reveals him to be as canny as a starship captain should be.

The old Romulan Admiral is portrayed in a sympathetic light, and the suicide of the Romulan at the conclusion adds a downbeat note to the victory of Picard over the Romulans in their showdown. There is a nice touch in the form of a letter the Romulan Admiral leaves behind for his wife and daughter, a communication which can only be delivered when the Romulans and the Federation at last declare a complete peace rather than an armed truce.

The concept of what to do with super-soldiers after the war is over is explored in "The Hunted." It's an interesting idea as it deals with a society that depended on these men to win a conflict for them, but this same society is then afraid to let them associate with normal people when the war is over in spite of the sacrifices these men made to preserve that society. In keeping with the principle of the Prime Directive, Picard ultimately refuses to solve the problem for them but insists that the planet and the soldiers work it out between them before that planet will be admitted to the Federation. This is a logical approach since this society will have to live with that decision and so must solve their own problems. It raises an interesting question though. Once a planet is in the Federation, if it has a revolution, which side would the Federation support if both sides appealed for aid? That very idea is dealt with in the next episode.

In one sense "The Hunted" seemed to be THE NEXT GENERATION's Vietnam episode just as "A Taste of Armageddon" was Classic Trek's Vietnam episode. Whereas "A Taste of Armageddon" dealt with endlessly fighting a war out of habit wherein no clear goals exist any longer, "The Hunted" is like a Vietnam aftermath story. When men are trained to kill and be the perfect soldier, where is their place in a peace time society when the war is over? This is a question that Vietnam veterans are still wrestling 20 years after the end of that conflict. So it remains a subject well worth exploring, even in a science fiction context.

BENDING THE PRIME DIRECTIVE

When Gene Roddenberry was honored by the Museum of Broadcasting in 1988, he stated that he wanted to deal with the subject of terrorists in a forthcoming episode, and demonstrate that even they have what they feel is a legitimate point of view. In the 1960's such a notion would have been considered impossibly radical for something like the old STAR TREK to have ever tackled.

In NEXT GENERATION this idea is wrestled with in "The High Ground," and while the terrorists' point of view is presented, they are nevertheless shown as going too far in their willingness to kill the innocent along with the guilty. This is essentially the 20th century earth conflict in Northern Ireland homogenized for consumer consumption and reduced to a very simplified form.

In describing what he hoped to accomplish, Roddenberry had stated, "What we want to do is to grapple now with the problems of the 80s and 90s and the turn of the century. I think we are going to surprise you on technology. You can only go so far in making things smaller and faster and more powerful. What other things should technology be worrying about? We're going to be getting into those areas. There's a reason to do another STAR TREK now. We did the original STAR TREK about the problems of the 60s. Many people forget that, in the mid-60s, when we put on a multi-racial crew, that was considered awful. People were shocked.

"Now we want to talk about hostage situations. I am amazed to see the hostage (takers) treated as bad guys always. Many of these people have legitimate complaints. The world is not as simple as we lay it out—good guys here, bad guys there. I am very concerned and want to find a way to get into the fact that most of the warfare and killing going on in the world is going on in the name of religion; organized religion. Not that I'm saying that there are not great plans and that we are not part of some great thing, but it is not the type of thing you see preached on television. I don't hold anyone up to ridicule. My mother is a good Baptist and she believes in many great things. But I cannot sit still in a series of this type and not point out who's killing who in the world."

The terrorists kidnap Picard and other Enterprise crewmen not because of anything they've actually done (other than tending wounded) but because they believe that Picard is going to side with the oppressive ruling class. With a little work, the complexities of such a situation could have been explored much better. Since this is a civil war at work here, the Federation actually chooses to help neither side in the conflict and is only drawn into it when their own personnel are kidnapped since the terrorists want to force the issue. But the terrorists are never portrayed with the sort of human dimension Roddenberry seemed to have in mind. They express no remorse or concerns over the consequences of their actions, but believe that the end justifies the means. It's been done before.

"Transfigurations" deals once again with the Enterprise being pushed and pulled into the middle of the affairs of another culture. This time Picard takes a stand, refusing to turn over an escaped criminal for what would clearly be

LEONARD
NIMOY AT
THE PRE-
MIERE OF
STAR TREK
VI.

execution, and it's the right decision. It's an interesting idea, dealing with the concept of a race evolving and those left behind attempting to destroy those who represent the actual future of their kind.

It also shows that the Prime Directive doesn't just provide an excuse for not getting involved or prohibiting someone from taking a moral stand. On the '60s STAR TREK, Captain Kirk's interpretation of the Prime Directive was clearly a loose one that allowed him to act on his own judgment rather than to turn and walk away while people slaughtered themselves in a useless civil conflict. The Federation is supposed to represent enlightened self-interest, not just self-interest. In spite of the many violations of the Prime Direction which Jim Kirk seemed guilty of, he would no doubt have had solid moral convictions behind each and every decision he made.

LITTLE OF CONSEQUENCE

Other third year Classic Trek episodes of note include "The Empath," "All Our Yesterdays," and even "The Paradise Syndrome" which has some nice touches in it. "The Paradise Syndrome" is the one where Captain Kirk becomes an Indian, but the story is nicely handled and the cinematography is superb. Like some other third year shows, it concluded on a solemn note as it closed with Kirk at the deathbed of his wife, Miramanee, with an expression of great sorrow on his face.

This scene elicits a very emphatic reaction from audiences when seen in a group on a large screen at a convention, because seeing the picture twenty times larger than the small screen you're used to seeing it on can be quite moving. "The Paradise Syndrome" was another episode which touched on the mystery of the Preservers, an unknown alien race whose mysterious seeding of planets with various humanoid races was not solved until the NEXT GENERATION episode "The Chase."

Another third season story, "Let That Be Your Last Battlefield" is as relevant and ham-handed as they come, as is "The Way To Eden." The first one deals with racism and arrives at the stunning, and supposedly surprising, conclusion that racism is bad. "The Way To Eden" is about futuristic Hippies who are misguided and come to a bad end. Only the first season NEXT GENERATION episode "Symbiosis" is as bad as either of these.

"Symbiosis" is a twist on the drug addiction story-lines common on television shows. In this case an entire planet is addicted to a drug supplied by another world, but the addicts think the drug is "medicine" to prevent them from dying of an ancient plague. The deaths actually come from withdrawal symptoms. This rather simple story, about one culture exploiting another purely for profit, turns into a critique of runaway capitalism rather than the anti-drug story it was intended to be.

THE SKY'S THE LIMIT

One of the myths surrounding the cancellation of STAR TREK in 1969 was that the show had run out of ideas. That just wasn't true. A starship which travels from planet to planet, discovering new societies and uncovering secrets about old ones is filled with great possibilities. As THE NEXT GENERATION cruised through its third season, instead of running out of ideas it was exploring the STAR TREK universe in different and exciting ways.

"Sins Of The Father" is a key episode in the continuing examination of Klingons and their culture. This one actually goes to the Klingon homeworld where Worf encounters a younger brother he'd believed long dead. The examination of Klingon politics is complex and interesting. Worf's decision to accept an unfair expulsion from his society for the betterment of all is nothing less than heroic and shows him to be a true Klingon.

Picard is with him when he goes to the Klingon homeworld and there are interesting scenes of life among the common Klingons. This is particularly interesting since we're accustomed to seeing only warriors. Based on the way Worf acts and with what we've been told up until now, one would have thought that everyone in Klingon society was part of the warrior class. Finding out that this isn't necessarily so makes Worf's later condemnations of non-warrior class Klingons in "Birthright" all that more unusual.

"Hollow Pursuits" tackles an obvious but untried idea using the holodeck. What if a crewman conjured up images of fellow crewmen in order to use and degrade them? While handled tastefully here, one can imagine the more unusual extremes this idea could be taken to. Crewman Barclay spends too much time in his fantasy world on the holodeck because he has trouble dealing with the real world and his job aboard the Enterprise.

Only his ability to solve a crisis by coming up with just the right idea enables him to start recognizing this and putting his own life in order. But it does raise the issue that the holodeck can be abused, a concept which before and since will only be dealt with in the confines of a holodeck malfunction. And yet what if someone deliberately used the holodeck for a bad end? It remains an idea unexplored, just as the concept of becoming addicted to the use of the holodeck has never been addressed.

DOUBLE TROUBLE—AGAIN

The notion of doubles on the Enterprise turns up again in the third year TNG episode "Allegiance." When an alien replaces Picard he's soon exposed because of his lack of Picard's judgment skills. Just as Kirk was kidnapped and replaced by a double in "What Are Little Girls Made Of?", so too do Enterprise personnel in the 24th century have to contend with kidnapping.

In "The Most Toys," Data is abducted under cover of his supposed destruction. Data is captured by a crazed collector in a plot all too reminiscent of something from BUCK ROGERS or SPACE: 1999. What elevates it above the dreary and the routine is the way it deals with the consequences of imprisonment and the ethical dilemma of Data finding it necessary to make a decision to kill even though it violates his own personal moral code. Data doesn't actually kill his captor, although the ending makes it clear that he fully intended to.

"The Most Toys" was originally to star David Rappaport as the villain. Halfway through shooting the diminutive performer made his first suicide attempt and was promptly replaced. All his scenes were reshot, although those who saw the original footage labeled Rappaport's performance as brilliantly menacing. Perhaps one day that last performance of Rappaport (he succeeded in a second suicide try a couple months later) will be seen.

THIRD SEASON WITH A SAD END

THE NEXT GENERATION episode "The Offspring" is a touching story which deals with what would happen if Data created another version of himself, which he dubs his "child." The Federation tries to take possession, just as they did with Data in "The Measure Of A Man," although why they seemed on the verge of getting away with it this time and not last time remains unresolved. The episode concludes with Data's "daughter" dying due to some sort of android stress.

"The Offspring" actually hearkens back to the third season Trek Classic episode "Requiem For Methuselah." In that story a woman Kirk falls in love with turns out to be an android. When Kirk and her creator, a man named Flint, fight over her affections, she cannot tolerate the pain and dies. In both cases we are led to understand that the androids developed the ability to feel emotions and these emotions became too powerful for their artificial systems to handle when confronted with stressful situations. Perhaps Data is fortunate that his android body is incapable of experiencing such feelings.

A moving scene wound up having a dual meaning in "Requiem For Methuselah." This was the final episode of STAR TREK broadcast on NBC when the series completed its network run in August 1969. While "Turnabout Intruder" was the last new episode scene, the series then entered a summer rerun period which climaxed with the second showing of "Requiem For Methuselah."

This was a fitting episode to conclude with as it had a very solemn ending in which Spock uses the Vulcan mind meld to help Kirk forget his pain. But while this was a fitting tribute to the demise of the series, the fans would not forget their pain so easily.

On that summer night in 1969, it seemed like STAR TREK was gone forever. Who would have imagined that not only would STAR TREK return a decade later, but that it would spawn a sequel series? Created by Gene Roddenberry, that spin-off series, THE NEXT GENERATION, would insure that his series would find a new audience in the new generation of TV viewers.

GROWTH OF THE NEXT GENERATION

The third season of NEXT GENERATION concludes on a cliffhanger which doesn't artificially force events into this all too abused angle. In "The Best Of Both Worlds," the Borg return as long feared, and the Enterprise is the only vessel on the scene to confront them. Picard is quickly kidnapped, transformed and absorbed into the Borg collective where he become Locutus.

The tension is thick, particularly when an Away Team beams aboard the Borg ship in an attempt to rescue Picard. That they fail is only one of the surprises in store here. A good episode which holds up well even after what has been done in the three years since it originally aired (always a vital measurement). This will no doubt be a best-seller when it finally makes it to the home video market.

SEASON FOUR

Once NEXT GENERATION entered its fourth season, it really was going where no man had gone before. The original STAR TREK had faded out after three seasons and in so doing had left a lot of ground uncovered and a lot of experiments untried. But once TNG passed the mark previously set by Classic Trek, the urgency to push on into new areas was stronger than ever.

The highly anticipated "The Best Of Both Worlds, Part 2" proved to be a fitting conclusion to the third season cliffhanger of NEXT GENERATION. When the Enterprise fails to stop the Borg ship, it speeds off towards Earth where a fleet of starships attempt to halt it, unsuccessfully. The scene when the Enterprise catches up to the battle site and sees dozens of wrecked starships drifting in space is truly awesome, although scenes like this which attempt to convey the power of huge vistas are largely diminished on the small screen.

The notion of the Enterprise standing up alone against a supremely powerful menace which is on an intercept course to Earth is, of course, similar to the plot of STAR TREK—THE MOTION PICTURE. The reasons the two menaces are going to Earth are quite different, though, as the Borg are a far more traditional enemy than the alien space probe V'ger which was going to Earth to search for its creator. In many respects "The Best of Both Worlds" had the kind of storyline which would have played much better as a feature film on the order of a STAR TREK motion picture.

The follow-up episode, "Family," chose not to ignore the consequences of what Picard has just gone through. While the rivalry between Picard and his older brother in their quaint French village seems forced and artificial (and all too easily resolved), other aspects of the reunion are rewarding, particularly the brief scenes between Picard and his young nephew. The actor who played his nephew would return two years later to play Picard when he's turned into a child in the sixth season episode "Rascals."

The fact that the show would do a character story which involved nothing more than people talking about their feelings demonstrated the chances the series is willing to take. Unfortunately "Family" was the lowest rated episode of the season, which says more about the audience than it does about the series.

NEXT GENERATION by its fourth season was perhaps where Classic Trek might have been in its fourth year, had there been one. Roddenberry had wanted to do episodes spotlighting characters more in the fourth season way back when as it had never really gotten around to telling us a great deal about the background of Jim Kirk.

Just as Jean-Luc Picard was able to make an idyllic trip back to a region of France untouched by the passage of the centuries, it would have been nice to see Captain Kirk return home to the Iowa town where he'd been raised. The '60s episode "The Menagerie" contains a scene in which Chris Pike is in a park-like setting on 23rd century Earth where a futuristic city can be seen far in the background.

What would Iowa have been like in the 23rd century? What kind of story could have been wrought around the hometown boy coming back to the old homestead and meeting people he hadn't seen since before he went off to Starfleet Academy? Sadly, due to the demands and styles of sixties television, Jim Kirk probably would have been called on to solve a murder mystery. After all, the original STAR TREK was supposed to be an action/adventure show and networks got twitchy back then if the drama became too introspective on its action fare.

THINGS ARE MORE THAN THEY SEEM

The original STAR TREK sometimes got bogged down trying to tell morality plays and do heavy handed social commentary. The fact that such episodes and little discussed or remembered just demonstrates their lack of success at doing something that self-conscious. Even NEXT GENERATION fell back on that in its first season in "Symbiosis," an anti-drug story.

"Suddenly Human," starts out like it's going to be a TNG story dealing with child abuse. Even the coming attractions made it out to be this kind of story. But actually it's nothing of the sort. In fact it could be regarded as being a story about how child abuse is assumed when it's not really there, and the complexity given to the issue is a welcome change.

When Picard discovers that a human child has been raised by the aliens who slew the boy's family eleven years before, the captain is determined to return him to his people. While Picard has some success drawing out the boy's human memories and reactions, in the end he realizes that in spite of the unfortunate circumstances, the boy belongs with the foster father who loved and raised him. It's an episode which asks difficult questions and provides difficult, and uncomfortable, answers. Frankly, Trek Classic never would have taken such a downbeat position as this story does, and that also shows the risks which NEXT GENERATION is willing to take.

"Remember Me" plays with reality in a manner which brings to mind the works of author Philip K. Dick. When Dr. Crusher notes that people she knows are no longer aboard the Enterprise, she finds it difficult to convince anyone else of this when no trace of the missing person's existence can be traced. We're over halfway through the story before we actually realize what's really going on and the pace sustains itself well.

HAIL AND FAREWELL

"Reunion" is another Klingon storyline. It continues the tradition of having episodes focusing on Worf which explore his Klingon character and heritage. These episodes have consistently been among the finest the series has produced. In this case Picard is dragged into things as well when the Klingon ritual of ascendancy to the throne is at hand. But it is the subterfuge behind-the-scenes which tells the tale.

Here we meet Worf's old lover and a son named Alexander (not exactly a Klingon name) that he never knew he had. The ending, when Worf decides to allow his adoptive parents to raise his own son just as they raised him, is quite touching and clearly leaves an opening for future stories. As it turns out, this episode marked what would be a downturn in the characterization of Worf, or what has been called the "domesticating" of the Klingon. Burdened by a son, Worf struts like a Klingon but wrongs his hands like any human father. Seeing Worf yelling at his son for not picking up after himself in forthcoming episodes is painful to see.

Another story about the nature of reality, which one could also say owes something to the influence of Philip K. Dick, is "Future Imperfect." This story is done so well that it keeps us guessing right up to the end. Even when we're congratulating ourselves for guessing that Riker is being tricked by a Romulan illusion, we never think that it could actually be an illusion within an illusion.

Episodes like "Future Imperfect" and "Remember Me" show the possible story directions never attempted by classic STAR TREK. The fact of the matter is that television science fiction tends to be ten to twenty years behind what is happening in the literature of science fiction. The books by Phil Dick which truly examined the nature of a person's perceived reality as opposed to actual reality didn't really appear until the '70s, and they were clearly influential tomes. In the '60s, Gene Roddenberry was still influenced by the science fiction of the '40s and '50s, as much as he tried to advance those ideas with the styles of drama television was doing in the '60s.

THINGS TO COME

Will Decker had a breakdown and did what he felt was necessary in the '60s STAR TREK episode "The Doomsday Machine." Captain Maxwell decides to use his starship to fight his own private war in the NEXT GENERATION episode "The Wounded."

In this story, a starship captain is convinced that the Cardassians are preparing for war again and decides to attack them first. Captain Maxwell had lost his family to the Cardassians in the previous war and refuses to see the miscreants launch another campaign of terror. The story is actually quite interesting and gives O'Brien a good scene since he served with Maxwell in the past and fought the Cardassians in the last war. The twist ending of having Picard figure out that Maxwell had guessed correctly, is a nice touch. Maxwell's mistake was that he launched a counteroffensive without sufficient proof and against Starfleet orders.

"The Wounded" would turn out to be a crucial episode as it introduced the Cardassians to the STAR TREK universe. As nasty as the Klingons ever were in Trek Classic, and even more ruthless than the Romulans (if that is possible), the Cardassians are the same kind of relentless, stereotyped villains Roddenberry later regretted creating in the form of the '60s version of the Klingons. Roddenberry later felt guilty about creating an entire race which was portrayed as being evil and did penance by reversing himself when he set down the rules for THE NEXT GENERATION.

The Cardassians, of course, formed a vital element of the background for DEEP SPACE NINE. The one-note villainy of them has also been broadened as an episode of DEEP SPACE NINE titled "Duet" featured a Cardassian who felt guilt for his race's war crimes and imitated a known war criminal in hopes that he would be tried for those crimes and thereby force his people to confront their collective guilt.

NEW IDEAS

"First Contact" is an episode of thrilling ideas. While the Prime Directive was established in Trek Classic, this episode more directly explores the notion of avoiding contact with societies not prepared to confront the reality of life on other worlds. When Riker, who is disguised as an alien, is injured on the surface of a planet in a freak accident, he is exposed when taken to a hospital. The resulting paranoia regarding an "alien invasion" threatens Riker's life. A variety of characters are presented, including a woman who wants to accompany Picard back to the Enterprise when Riker is rescued, as well as an official who is terrified of what the existence of the Enterprise represents to their future.

Trek Classic never approached the idea of first contact in this complicated a fashion. While the story is diminished somewhat by the Bebe Neuwirth character who wants to "have sex with an alien," the rest of the story takes the high road. This episode demonstrates the drama of ideas.

In Classic Trek, "Court Martial" put Captain Kirk on the defensive when he was accused of murder. In "The Drumhead," Picard finds that he and certain personnel on the Enterprise are under suspicion based on the flimsiest of evidence. Jean Simmons as J'Dan is excellent in this story which demonstrates that the Federation isn't all squeaky clean.

Picard's character has finally emerged as a strong commander since the second season, and in "The Drumhead" he essentially must go up against Starfleet. That the Federation might have a dark side was never touched on in Classic Trek. Actually, David Gerrold did propose such an idea in his original story outline for "The Enterprise Incident" in 1968. Originally he had Captain Kirk undertake the spy mission and then denounce Starfleet for engaging in such immoral activity. The fact that a hero following orders might not be the right thing to do was not a notion the producer of STAR TREK was interested in pursuing back then.

A STRONG FEMALE ROLE

In Classic STAR TREK, Majel Barrett played two roles. First she appeared as Number One in the first pilot, "The Cage." In that role she played the character as though she were a Vulcan before the unemotional concept of Vulcans was grafted onto Spock. When NBC objected to the portrayal of a strong female character who was second in command, she was given a blond wig and played the shrinking violet Nurse Christine Chapel for three years. It was a bit of a comedown, but she was still on the Enterprise.

As Roddenberry told it, when he came up with the concept of Lwaxana Troi, he told his wife, "I've got a great character for you to play, and you don't even have to act!" The fact that the mother of Deanna Troi is usually written as a loud, obnoxious harridan tends to bleed the humor out of that joke, in spite of the fact that Gene Roddenberry is the one who told it.

Lwaxana Troi, as played by Majel Barrett, has been one of those characters one either finds amusing or obnoxious. Until her appearance in "Half A Life," the character has certainly never been very interesting. But the cartoon characterization of her was abandoned in that episode in which she falls in love with a man who is honor bound by his society to commit ritual suicide when he reaches the age of mandatory retirement. For him to refuse would bring horrible dishonor on his family.

THE DOCTOR STEPS OUT

By the fourth season of TNG the female roles were being written much better. Beverly Crusher was beginning to get more serious screen time and in "The Host" she was shown to be a mature woman who was also capable of having a stimulating love life. "The Host" is another episode which introduces an element which would become a part of DEEP SPACE NINE. Here we meet a Trill for the first time, an alien which can enter and merge with a host body. When the Trill's current host body is injured, it relocates for a time into Riker. The twist is that Dr. Crusher had been having an affair with the Trill in its previous host body.

The ending caused some controversy. When the Trill's new permanent host body turns out to be female, Crusher breaks off the affair. She certainly didn't have that objection when the Trill made love to her in Riker's body, something he certainly hadn't consented to when he offered to help save the Trill's life.

Dr. Crusher on NEXT GENERATION is shown to have much more of a personal life than Dr. McCoy ever had on

Classic Trek. The only romance McCoy ever on air was in the third season episode "For The World Is Hollow And I Have Touched The Sky." When the Enterprise encounters a generation ship, McCoy's falls in love with a woman he meets there.

A LANDMARK SEASON

Although Gene Roddenberry rarely granted interviews during his NEXT GENERATION days, he was quoted in the LOS ANGELES TIMES for Oct. 28th, 1990 on the occasion of the new series surpassing the 79 episode marker that the original STAR TREK TV series had achieved in the '60s.

Roddenberry also discussed the whole STAR TREK phenomenon in more depth, in particular as it related to THE NEXT GENERATION stating, "Many people haven't thought deeply what it is they like about it. They're not crazy about rocket ships or space travel. It's none of those things. What our show does, we take humanity maybe a century into the future. Our people do not lie, cheat or steal. They are the best of the best. When you watch the show, you say to yourself, at least once, 'My God, that's the way life should be!' "

As with season three, this season also featured a final episode cliffhanger. "Redemption, Part I" involves a power play on the Klingon home world. Worf takes a leave of absence to join in the conflict and serve on a Klingon ship commanded by his brother. Worf's aim is also to restore the good name of his family which was besmirched when his dead father was accused of collaborating with Romulans against his own people. It's a good, complicated story worthy of being the season finale.

Roddenberry clearly made good on his promise to turn the Klingons into characters who were not just cartoon bad guys. All through the '70s he regretted featuring such creative shortcuts and when he had the chance to make up for it he want all the way. His fellow writers and producers on NEXT GENERATION also saw the many possibilities inherent in creating a rich heritage and culture for the Klingons.

Possibly Roddenberry was also stung at seeing the Klingons played as simplistic villains once more in 1984 in STAR TREK III—THE SEARCH FOR SPOCK. In spite of Roddenberry's consulting status on the films he couldn't stand in the way of Leonard Nimoy's decission to feature the Klingons as the villains. Harve Bennett had originally intended using the Romulans. And so Roddenberry had seen Klingons portrayed as being even more brutal and brutish than he had used them back in the '60s. The Klingons had indeed been bruised and abused over the years and deserved a more complete portrayal than what one would expect to see in a Saturday morning cartoon.

SEASON FIVE

Roddenberry had little day to day contact with NEXT GENERATION by the time season five went into production, plus he was recovering from the first of two debilitating strokes. By this time Michael Piller and Rick Berman were producing the show and following the style and philosophy Roddenberry had established for the series.

Unlike Classic Trek, NEXT GENERATION was not an action/adventure show, nor had it ever been promoted as one. It had been promoted as STAR TREK, a science fiction series capable of being many things. The fifth year of TNG proved that, in spades.

Improved characterization and the exploration of ideas in a dramatic fashion had enabled NEXT GENERATION to grow and mature until the space battles and wild special effects of the STAR TREK motion pictures were not expected in every episode of NEXT GENERATION.

Captain Picard had developed into a rich personality with a cool head in a crisis and years of experience to draw on in any given situation. He would tend to approach a crisis intellectually whereas James T. Kirk would have approached it emotionally. Kirk commanded from gut instinct. Picard would adopt a wait and see attitude, not allowing himself to act prematurely in spite of obvious provocation.

Will Riker had learned much as Picard's first officer and his experience had taught him caution. In some ways he was like Spock, Kirk's first officer, as Riker weighed options carefully and studied his opponent while resisting the use of force except in the most extreme situations.

Data had come aboard the Enterprise as just another officer, and an android at that. But his search for the riddle of humanity had endeared him to many, and in spite of his lack of true emotions, Data clearly has a personality.

As Geordi matures he is beginning to have more and more in common with a certain former Enterprise engineer named Montgomery Scott. Geordi would dispute this, particularly after their encounter in the sixth season. But Geordi has done more than learn his way around an engine room. He has learned that the more complicated the technology, the more that can go wrong as well as the more that can be discovered and learned. He has learned to innovate in ways he would have considered impossible four years earlier.

Worf has learned that there is more to being a Klingon than just adopting the heritage. He must also live that heritage and accept the consequences. Worf has been to the Klingon homeworld more than once and also fought for redemption, which he achieved in the premiere episode of the fifth season. But Worf is torn between the peaceful goals of Starfleet and the warrior heritage of his ancestry that decrees that to die in battle is the highest honor one can attain.

THE THINKING MAN'S COMMANDER

Season five started to move in some more experimental directions beginning with "Darmok." That unusual episode deals with a race which spoke only in metaphors. Using an element seen previously in the Trek Classic episode "Arena," the captains of the Enterprise and an alien vessel meet face to face on the surface of a planet in order to settle their differences. It's a very unusual and satisfying story, although the average TV viewer may well have found it a bit difficult to follow due to the notion of communication through metaphors.

Although elements of the Trek Classic episode "Arena" have been borrowed by NEXT GENERATION before, here they are used in a way which is entirely fresh and original. Jean-Luc Picard has been elevated in status over five seasons to an intellectual. He is now so different from Jim Kirk that we literally cannot imagine Kirk faced with an alien and being forced to intellectualize his way out of the situation the way Picard finally does in "Darmok." Kirk is a commander for a more dangerous time while Picard is the ambassador of the future. One has the feeling that were Picard to have been able to spend more time with Spock in "Reunification," that the two would have doubtless found that they had a great deal in common.

A NEW CAST MEMBER

The only new cast member that Trek Classic introduced to the regular crew was Ensign Chekov. Walter Koenig was ostensibly brought aboard to appear to younger audiences and in many instances his character was treated as comedy relief.

NEXT GENERATION brought its own new ensign aboard the Enterprise in the popular episode "Ensign Ro" which introduced Michelle Forbes as the controversial Bajoran. Released from a Federation prison in order to assist the Enterprise on a vital mission, the story becomes increasing complex as Ro finds herself manipulated by a Federation admiral who has a secret deal with the Cardassians. In this one episode Ro is established as being a very interesting character and one who is a welcome addition to the Enterprise crew.

Ro Laren was the first serious move to bring a character aboard the Enterprise who did not entirely reflect the ideals of Gene Roddenberry. She didn't get along wither everyone and actually elicited dissension in the crew. When Picard offered her a permanent position on the Enterprise, it was over Riker's objections. He didn't think she was very good at following orders. He also didn't approve of her background. She was written well, though and was a fascinating character to see. Ensign Ro was more headstrong than belligerent and meshed surprisingly well with Geordi LaForge, a character who seems very much her opposite.

Michelle Forbes appeared in several more episodes in the fifth season as a semi-regular. She was slated to be a regular on DEEP SPACE NINE but her character had been written in without ever consulting her. When she turned down the series slot, Paramount representatives were reportedly so angry that they banned her from the Paramount lot. She appeared in only one sixth season episode in spite of the other actors on the show wanting to see her return.

Her absence from the series has been sorely felt. Whenever she has been given a large role, she steals every scene she's in. This is because her character has an edge to it and she's not afraid to argue with someone, something which even Worf doesn't do much any more.

WESLEY DEPARTS, SPOCK RETURNS

Wesley Crusher appeared in two episodes this season, "The Game" and "The First Duty," and in the second of the two the character was taken down a few notches. In "The Game," Wesley figures out that the Enterprise is being invaded and conquered by an insidious new game which addicts a part of the brain. Although Data saves everyone, that's only because Wesley reactivated Data after he had been shut down to insure he couldn't interfere.

In "The First Duty" the story is set at Starfleet Academy where Wesley is a real hotshot nearing graduation. When he becomes involved in a cover-up involving the death of one of his friends, Wesley's pristine image comes crashing down. Even though he finally confesses, it is clearly under duress and isn't something he would have done without outside pressure from Captain Picard. Since his public humiliation in "The First Duty," Wesley has not reappeared.

Year Five also marked the long rumored crossover of Mr. Spock on THE NEXT GENERATION in the two-part "Unification." While the story seemed a bit weak in part two, it still had some interesting moments throughout, although few of them involved Spock. The episode had a rushed feeling to the script as though the story was hastily concocted in order to get it into production to air in the November "sweeps month" ratings period early in the season. It achieved the ratings success it set out to accomplish, but dramatically the story left a lot to be desired.

This storyline also features the death of Sarek, which happens off-stage. Spock represented the entire concept of Trek Classic meeting THE NEXT GENERATION, but the two really do little more than shake hands. In spite of the long shadow cast by Spock, he's upstaged by the plotlines involving the NEXT GENERATION regulars.

It should be noted that Mark Lenard only appeared in one episode of the '60s STAR TREK as Sarek but bettered that by playing Spock's father in two NEXT GENERATION outings. In fact the first dramatic crossover between the two series occurred with the episode "Sarek." Mark Lenard is a fine actor who is rarely given material which shows off his abilities.

In both "Sarek" and "Reunification I," Lenard played a Vulcan in the throes of the debilitating Ben Dye syndrome, a disease which strikes Vulcans where it hurts them the most, by forcing them into exhibiting violent outbursts of emotions. Lenard's portrayal of the proud Sarek drifting in and out of anger and lucidity is a wonder to behold. In was a more demanding portrayal of the Vulcan than he'd been allowed to do way back in the '60s.

DATA AND EVIL PERSONIFIED

The character of Data has been explored in many ways, often to show the contrasts between him and the humans he works with. But in "Hero Worship" Data shows that he understands human psyche better than was thought as he is able to guide a young boy through a traumatic situation and out the other side again. When the boy loses his parents in an accident aboard a ship which the Enterprise finds drifting in space, the child blames himself. In order to escape the guilt and pain, he begins to imitate Data since androids don't feel pain. The teleplay by Joe Menosky is very sensitively and intelligently handled and is one of the strongest episodes of year five, a season which contained many strong episodes.

"Hero Worship" is also another twist on Data's search for what it means to be human. Confronted with a human who wants to be an android, Data examines both the elements that make him different from the boy, as well as those things he has in common. Ultimately it is Data who guides the boy back to his own humanity. It is the kind of well crafted story and bravura performances, portrayed with subtlety and imagination, which show just how far the NEXT GENERATION has come since its seemingly long ago first season.

"Conundrum" is an excellent mystery episode as the memories of the Enterprise crew are all selectively blanked and they are led to believe they are at war with the Lysians. One amusing sequence has Worf deciding that he must be the captain since he's the only Klingon aboard the Enterprise.

Interesting tricks are played with the characters in this one. While their personalities remain intact, they don't initially remember who they are or what their relationships are to one another. Thus Commander Riker and Ensign Ro, who normally can barely tolerate one another, strike up a fast friendship and even have a quick romance. Riker's reaction when he regains his memory and realizes what he has done is priceless. Again, its the characters, playing off each other and even against expectations, that elevates this storyline beyond being just a basic double-blind mystery.

Characterization playing against expectations makes "Power Play" a powerful episode indeed. When Data, O'Brien and Troi are taken over by alien entities, they ruthlessly try to take over the Enterprise so that they can rescue their fellow entities marooned on the planet the ship is orbiting. Marina Sirtis is shown that she actually has range as a performer as she is apparently taken over by a male alien who is the brutal leader of those who had been exiled on the world below. She displays a nonstop thread of anger and viciousness as takes control of the situation and refuses to relent right up until the moment she faces defeat.

Troi becomes a character who is dangerous and we believe it absolutely. While seeing Data and O'Brien playing similar personalities is also a kick, we've seen this before with Data when his "evil twin" was around. The ending on the story seems a little convenient but overall it's a captivating episode which is just as powerful in subsequent viewings.

POINT OF VIEW

Worf was all but domesticated this season when his son Alexander returned to live on the Enterprise in "The New Ground." Seeing Worf more as a father than a warrior dilutes much of the edge this character has had up until this season. This episode almost marked the death knell for this character as no excellent Klingon episodes were made in the fifth season and it wouldn't be until close to the end of season six that the old Worf would re-emerge.

"Ethics" is more-or-less a Klingon episode in which Worf suffers a crippling spine injury due to a freak accident. Because we know that Worf will recover, everything that happens seems by the numbers. The only interesting touches are when Worf demands the right to commit suicide rather than live on as a cripple. Riker refuses to help him and points out that by Klingon law the oldest son must commit the killing, something Worf cannot bring himself to let Alexander do.

This episode just points out the pitfalls of trying to do something traumatic to a regular cast member to whom writers are forbidden to do anything permanent to. It once again reminds one of the Classic Trek episode "For The World Is Hollow And I Have Touched The Sky" in which Dr. McCoy temporarily had a terminal disease.

The most controversial episode of the season was "The Outcast." This is a story of an alien race where some members realize they are sexually different from their fellow androgens. In spite of how damn careful the script writer strived to be, some people were still offended by the story's plea for compassion and its slam against prejudice which seemed to strike a bit too close to home.

But in twenty-six years of STAR TREK, it is easily the bravest story the series has ever told. And yet by having the androgen race portrayed entirely by actresses, it make the condemnation of one of their member's involvement with Riker come across as a race of Lesbians condemning relations with men. It tries hard, but by being too careful it creates new pitfalls for itself.

Time travel gets a new STAR TREK twist in "Cause And Effect." This time the Enterprise is caught in a time loop which begins repeating each time the starship is destroyed. What could have been boring and repetitious was actually fascinating, and the direction of Jonathan Frakes shows that he has a firm grasp on what the series is really about. The episode begins with the time loop and the destruction of the Enterprise and then after the commercial break picks up at the beginning of the loop again. What makes it all work is that events don't repeat exactly, but rather there are differences and coincidences that the crew begin to notice in spite of having no conscious memory of the previous time loop experience. It's another experimental episode which is fascinating to watch.

The wonders of time travel were established in STAR TREK back in the '60s in "Tomorrow Is Yesterday" when the Enterprise went back in time by accident. Time travel was explored by classic Trek in a different manner in "The City On The Edge Of Forever." But by the time "Assignment: Earth" appeared late in the second season, the Enterprise knew how to time travel on purpose. That process is the same one used by Kirk and crew in STAR TREK IV—THE VOYAGE HOME. They called it "the slingshot effect."

DATA'S HEAD

The Borg were presented in a different light when "I, Borg" showed one which was capable of human compassion. This may well lead to changing the one-note characterizations of these villains into something more complicated. This episode has also formed the background for events which began to unfold in the season six cliffhanger as "Hugh" the Borg reappears at the beginning of season seven.

This all may have been done because until this episode, the Borg had been portrayed as being one-note villains on the order of the Klingons circa the 1960's. Remembering those lessons learned from watching old STAR TREK, someone apparently decided to explore the Borg in more than simple and obvious ways. The result is a fascinating exercise in exploring the nature of humanity in ways different than Data has on the android front.

But when it comes to experimentation, fans are still discussing "Inner Light." When Captain Picard is zapped by an alien space probe, he is seemingly drawn a thousand years into the past where he lives out the remainder of his life as a husband and father, only to reawaken on the Enterprise and find that he's been unconscious for 20 minutes!

And finally, the season cliffhanger, "Time's Arrow" got us hooked with a story which presumably told us how Data will die. Rather than a battle story such as the cliffhangers from seasons three and four offered, this was a more complicated story involving 19th century San Francisco, Mark Twain, Guinan before she'd ever met anyone on the Enterprise, and strange aliens stealing the life force from humans in the past. The

WALTER KOENIG AT THE STAR TREK SIGNATURE CEREMONY AT THE MANN CHINESE THEATRE ON DECEMBER 5, 1991.

© 1991 Ortega/Galell a Ltd.

episode is sometimes referred to by fans as "Data's Head," a parody of the Trek Classic episode title "Spock's Brain."

The one NEXT GENERATION character about which the least is known is Guinan. "Time's Arrow" features Guinan more than any other episode next to "Yesterday's Enterprise." She comments on the action, makes suggestions about the action and consoles the participants but rarely becomes involved herself. What we know about Guinan can be ticked off on one hand. She hates Q (as revealed in "Q Who") and she comes from a world destroyed by the Borg, as revealed in that same episode. "Time's Arrow" reveals where and how she first met Jean-Luc Picard when she was visiting Earth and San Francisco in the 19th century, and she apparently was not time traveling. Guinan is a conundrum wrapped in a mystery. As Whoppi Goldberg put it, she knows Guinan's secrets, but she's not telling.

Overall, season five turned out to be one of the best seasons yet and promised high hopes for year six. It presented STAR TREK adventures far different than the realms explored by Roddenberry and his staff in the '60s. This is because science fiction has expanded into many other realms of sociology and ideas in the twenty years since the original STAR TREK ended its run. Plus there were a lot of things Gene Roddenberry wanted to do with STAR TREK in the '60s which he never had the opportunity to try. His successors are now following his lead and exploring the creative avenues which were closed to Gene after the first STAR TREK was canceled in 1969.

SEASON SIX

Year six got off to a rocky start with the extremely disappointing conclusion to "Time's Arrow." The meandering storyline in part 2 completely undercut all of the excitement established in the first part as it lurched from one scene to another, dragging Samuel Clemens along for the unnecessary ride. The build-up to part two turned into a big letdown as the alien life-force thieves were never given any personality beyond being the bad guys.

While all of the loose ends are tied up, it is done in a very by the numbers manner with not a single clever twist or turn. The presence of Samuel Clemens is so disposable that were one to go through and cut him completely out of the script, the story would turn out exactly the same, for while the other characters acknowledge Twain's presence, he doesn't have any real affect on the plot!

The interesting characters and the clever twists and turns wrought on them in so many of the fifth season NEXT GENERATION episodes seemed to have been overlooked or forgotten as the sixth year got under way.

By the time the sixth year came to an end there were nearly twice as many episodes of NEXT GENERATION as there had been of Classic Trek. When people wonder why the old STAR TREK is becoming overlooked and pushed into the background, this is why. The sheer volume of episodes featuring the NEXT GENERATION gang has opened up vistas which the original STAR TREK just never had the opportunity to explore.

Classic STAR TREK had planned a fourth season episode which featured Dr. McCoy's daughter, Joanna, but it just never came to pass. On NEXT GENERATION we've not only seen Dr. Crusher's son Wesley grow up, but have experienced the highs and lows in his life along the way.

When the original STAR TREK characters were granted a life extension into the motion picture arena, it was to explore the cosmos and everything that's grand about it. The small moments, the precious times, just weren't big enough for the big screen.

In STAR TREK—THE MOTION PICTURE, Spock learns to laugh. He discovers that being devoid of emotion is not the end all and be all he thought it was. That's actually the most interesting part of the film and that small scene forms an important link to its TV series routes. In STAR TREK II—THE WRATH OF KHAN, a space battle and the death of Spock create an explosive story which is almost operatic in its size and power.

STAR TREK III—THE SEARCH FOR SPOCK deals with nothing less than the resurrection of Spock, the death of Kirk's son, the destruction of the Enterprise as well as the destruction of the Genesis planet. But it's the little moments, the scene at the end when Spock recognizes Kirk that touch us. We never watched STAR TREK for explosions and melodrama, but to see the imaginative landscape Kirk, Spock and the others would explore.

It's for that reason that STAR TREK IV—THE VOYAGE HOME is regarded as being closer to the roots of Classic Trek than any of the other films because it is an idea driven story propelled by the characters. It seems to be a smaller story compared with the others, but it's a larger story on a personal level. "I work in space but I'm from Iowa," says Kirk. Yes. This is STAR TREK!

STAR TREK V seemed to be an imitation of what the movies had made STAR TREK, while STAR TREK VI—THE UNDISCOVERED COUNTRY formed a vital link between old STAR TREK and new. The Klingon Armistice. This is the beginning of THE NEXT GENERATION. Its roots lie there.

OLD ACQUAINTANCES

Surprisingly, Scotty's crossover appearance on THE NEXT GENERATION in "Relics" is better written than Spock's was in "Reunification." James Doohan is actually given some acting to do for a change, particularly in the portrayal of him as a man out of time—an old man who just doesn't fit into the new world he's been brought into. The fact that he finds a way to fit in at the end opens up possibilities for the future, particularly now that Paramount is planning another STAR TREK television spin-off. The scene fans are still talking about is the holodeck scene when Scotty resurrects the bridge of the original starship Enterprise. It is an amazing thing to see again. In the novelization of "Relics," the author added elements to the holodeck scene, including Scotty talking to Kirk and Spock.

"True Q" managed to come up with a new twist on the old reprobate when a woman stationed aboard the Enterprise reveals that she has fantastic powers. The reason she does is that her father was a Q who fell in love with a human. The resulting child grew up an orphan, following the mysterious death of her parents. While Q tries to get the young woman to agree to become a Q with the others, Picard determines that her parents were actually executed by the Q for refusing a directive from them.

It's a change of pace Q episode and works well. In some respects the child with fantastic powers is something of a throwback to "Charlie X" in the '60s, but the young woman in "True Q" is not portrayed as a misfit, although she does have moments in which she must question the proper use of her powers. The problem with Charlie in that Classic Trek episode was that he'd never learned about ethics or restraint, and was therefore doomed to live out his days powerful but alone. The woman in "True Q" has a very different future in store for her.

CHARACTER THROWBACKS

Season six was a season of continued episodes and the first of these was the 2-part story "Birthright." During a visit to Deep Space Nine, Worf encounters a man who offers to sell Worf information about the whereabouts of his Klingon father. Worf forces the information from the man and it leads to a moon under the control of Romulans. It is a prison planet where Klingon prisoners have grown old and their children have grown up unaware of many of the old Klingon customs. It's an interesting story which gives Worf the chance to act like a true Klingon for the first time in two years. On the other hand it shows up the dichotomy in Worf's thinking—he's a member of Starfleet, which represents peace, but he's offended when he encounters Klingons who aren't warlike. Must all Klingons live to fight and kill? Someone has convinced Worf that they should, and he accepts this unquestioningly. Is Worf becoming a throwback to the Klingons of the 1960's?

This was also the season which decided to show that Captain Kirk wasn't the only Enterprise commander who was a man of action. "Starship Mine," in which Picard finds himself trapped aboard the Enterprise between two deadly points of opposition, is clearly DIE HARD on a starship. Picard, alone on the ship when he discovers criminals stealing a deadly waste-product for use in a weapon, must both battle and elude them.

Complicating the matter is a lethal decontamination ray slowly sweeping the length of the supposedly evacuated starship. Picard resorts to weapons both new and old as he proves himself to be just as ruthless as the criminals he's up against. Just as interesting is a scene in which Data hears about a boring diplomat whom he deliberately engages in pointless conversation to learn how to talk endlessly without saying anything worth listening to. It's quite a funny scene, especially if you're a fan of well thought out verbal humor.

KEY EPISODES

Some fans have expressed disappointment with year six overall, but were one to sit down and go through the season episode by episode, it clearly emerges as being at least as good as season five. There are some weak episodes here and there but many strong ones as well, including some which are quite imaginative.

"The Chase" has so much in the storyline that it could have easily been stretched into a two part adventure. Thankfully it wasn't as it is written tightly and works perfectly as a single episode thriller. The reason it works is that it features no subplots to slow things down.

"Chains of Command," an unusual 2-part episode, introduces a replacement for Picard who manages to get on Riker's bad side. When Picard is sent on an espionage mission, it turns out to be a Cardassian trick. But even more, Picard is tortured in sequences which give Patrick Stewart the chance to present some of the finest acting he's ever done. That his work in THE NEXT GENERATION for this season wasn't nominated for an Emmy is inexplicable.

This episode also demonstrates that humanity in the 24th century isn't as perfect as Roddenberry claimed. Ronny Cox, as the new Captain of the Enterprise, and Riker don't see eye to eye at all and continually clash over styles of command. The new captain even labels Riker unfit to be a First Officer, which is quite a switch.

A SEQUEL FIVE YEARS LATER

"Ship In A Bottle" is the long awaited sequel to the first year episode "Elementary Dear Data." In that earlier episode, Data had the holodeck create Professor Moriarty, the notorious enemy of Sherlock Holmes, and then gave him all of the android's knowledge in order to create a worthy adversary.

The only problem is that now the hologram of Moriarty knows it's a hologram and is determined to hold on to its existence at any price.

By using Moriarty twice, STAR TREK used the character even more than Doyle did! Legends being what they are, not everyone realizes that Prof. Moriarty appeared in only one Sherlock Holmes story—"The Final Problem." But he was such a well rendered character, complete with a detailed criminal background, that Moriarty was used time and again in Holmes movies and elsewhere years after Doyle died.

But while Doyle portrayed Moriarty as a black-hearted villain, on THE NEXT GENERATION he is something more than that. Moriarty becomes a man obsessed with remaining alive and who exhibits human feelings of love and compassion. But he's still willing to go to seemingly any length to preserve his existence. A contradiction exists in this episode in that while Data argues for recognizing true life in the droids in "The Quality of Life," Moriarty clearly qualifies for this even more as he is aware of his own existence and is more than just a program on the holodeck. "Ship In A Bottle" has many interesting twists and turns, particularly the conclusion. While a sequel may one day be done to this episode as well, it would be unnecessary. Though done 5 years apart, these two TNG episodes form a perfect, self-contained whole.

Moriarty may be regarded by some as NEXT GENERATION's answer to Khan Noonian Sing, the '60s STAR TREK villain who met his end in STAR TREK II—THE WRATH OF KHAN. But Moriarty is a little more complicated than that. When Data created this character in the holodeck, he apparently did not really try to infuse Moriarty with the same villainy he had in Doyle's story.

The Moriarty seen in those two NEXT GENERATION episodes is single-minded, but also capable of honor and compassion. He just doesn't want to return to the oblivion from which Data created him. It would thus be a mistake for THE NEXT GENERATION to resurrect Moriarty as some sort of major villain in a motion picture the way STAR TREK did with Khan when they revived the character introduced in "Space Seed" in 1967. Moriarty and Khan are two very different characters. Just because someone is an antagonist it doesn't follow that they are also a villain.

THE SUPPORTING CAST ALSO RISES

Early in its original run, the '60s STAR TREK did episodes which spotlighted one character by building a story around them. "The Man Trap" is a McCoy episode while "The Galileo Seven" put Spock in the spotlight, and under close examination, for the first time. But the supporting characters, such as Sulu, Uhura and Chekov, never got this opportunity. Had Classic Trek continued into a fourth season, Roddenberry had intended to make up for that oversight. NEXT GENERATION did finally pick up on that idea after a few seasons and year six featured some excellent examples of giving the supporting roster their moment in the sun.

The character of Troi has never been given an episode built around her which was particularly interesting. The closest TNG had ever come was in "Power Play" which showed what the actress could do when given something more substantial to work with. But she was finally given something substantial in "Face Of The Enemy." The teaser when Troi awakens and discovers that she has been turned into a Romulan shows that we're in for something pretty unusual. The episode doesn't let us down as it takes us aboard a Romulan ship and shows us what life among the Romulans is like. No episode since "Balance of Terror" has done anything even remotely like this about the Romulans. It's quite impressive. Equally impressive is that Marina Sirtis demonstrates that she's clearly up to the demands of the material.

Dr. Crusher gets her own episode in "Suspicions," a story which is more interesting for some of the secondary elements than for its primary murder mystery. For the first time we meet a Ferengi scientist, and he's completely unlike the Ferengi businessmen and starship personnel we've met up until now. Another interesting touch is that a shuttle in the episode is named the "Justman," a reference to Bob Justman, a producer on the '60s STAR TREK.

The fifth year episode, "Ethics," made much of Dr. Crusher's unwillingness to cross the line when it comes to medical treatment. But in "Suspicions" when the Ferengi scientist is killed, Beverly insists she has to perform an autopsy, but Picard forbids it. Such a thing is against the religion of the scientist's family. Medical ethics should have forbidden her from proceeding, but finally she violates the rules—and promptly faces suspension. This seems somewhat inconsistent with the hard-nosed ethicist Beverly came across as in the episode "Ethics" as here she breaks the rules because it is the expedient thing to do, which is exactly the attitude she had condemned in the earlier episode. But then reportedly Gates McFadden hadn't been entirely happy with how her character had been written in "Ethics" because of how by the book she was there.

KLINGON OVERCOMPENSATION

"Rightful Heir" deals with the biological resurrection of Kahless, an ancient Klingon warrior who is legendary among even the modern warriors. Because of what Worf encountered in "Birthright" when he met Klingons who were out of touch with their past, Worf has been feeling inadequate and trying to get closer to his own heritage. This leads him to the world where Kahless promised to return to, and Worf is just in time to witness the resurrection.

The scene when Worf threatens to kill Koroth and the Guardians on the spot if they don't admit the truth about the origin of Kahless shows that Worf isn't a wimp any more. Lest you think that the idea for Kahless was just pulled out of the air, a very different version of the character was originally done in the third season Trek Classic episode "The Savage Curtain."

NEW TWISTS

In the Trek Classic blooper reel there's a scene from 1966 where a 10 year old boy wearing pointed ears walks onto the bridge and says to Mr. Spock, "Hi, daddy." That child was Leonard Nimoy's son, Adam. Twenty-seven years later, Adam Nimoy, an entertainment attorney turned director, is at the helm of "Timescape," one of the more challenging episodes of the sixth season. In "Timescape" the destruction of the Enterprise takes place again, but time is manipulated in a different manner.

The directing by Adam Nimoy is quite good, particularly in light of the complicated requirements of the story. This episode is both suspenseful and imaginative and keeps you guessing right up to the climax. It's quite an accomplishment.

Picard has certainly had plenty of starring venues in TNG but nothing like "Tapestry." When Picard is the victim of an assassination attempt, he apparently dies—and meets Q. Does this mean that Q is God, or something along those lines? Q even gives Picard the chance to relive part of his life as well as to endure the consequences. The ending leaves the story open to interpretation as to whether Picard was hallucinating or not, particularly since Q doesn't reappear after Picard awakens.

DATA AND THE BORG

In the '60s, the only TV shows with cliffhangers were shows like LOST IN SPACE. While they told a complete story in one episode, they would then show the teaser of the next episode as the end of the show in order to hook you into coming back next week. Classic Trek never went this route and in fact the only two-part show they ever did, "The Menagerie," appeared in the first half of the first season. It never occurred to them to come up with a story which people would have to wait four months to see the outcome of. But times change.

Since the end of season three, THE NEXT GENERATION has been striving to craft cliffhangers which would keep the viewing audience on the edge of their seats throughout the summer as they awaited the fall premiere. This has never been better accomplished than with "Descent," the sixth season climax. While setting us up for the return of "Hugh" the Borg from the fifth season, we instead encounter Lore, Data's "evil twin" last seen in the fourth season. Just when we'd practically forgotten about the miscreant, he returns, and in the worst way possible —leading a contingent of the Borg.

Data began acting strangely earlier in year six when he began having a recurring dream in "Birthright." Then in "Descent" Data actually becomes angry during a fight with the Borg, an emotion he is surprised to have since Data has never exhibited any true emotions before. Data works at duplicating the experience in order to better understand its origins. This is important to Data, of course, because he has been trying to discover the secret of emotions for years.

Data knows that he felt genuine anger and thereby exhibited a human emotion. If he can discover how he locked into that feeling it could reveal the path to other genuine human emotions. Is Data on the verge of achieving his goal? The android has sometimes been compared with Pinocchio, the wooden creation who wanted to be a real boy. Will Data finally perform that one deed which will lead to the gift of humanity? The seventh, and final, year of THE NEXT GENERATION will tell the tale.

On the other hand Spock spent a lifetime denying his humanity and searching for the key to Vulcan perfection. In STAR TREK—THE MOTION PICTURE Spock neared that goal, only to discover that it was not so desirable a thing to have after all. In many respects Data has proven his "humanity" over and over again in the way he has treated others and the insights he has shown in the behavior of the people around him.

In six years THE NEXT GENERATION has accomplished a great deal and this was well exemplified in season six. Although Roddenberry had frozen the show into an unrealistic idealism where the crew of the Enterprise existed in perfect and absolute harmony, "Chain of Command" aptly demonstrated just how that harmony could be ruptured.

This one episode showed many of the unrealized potentials that still exist in the characters on the series and may well point in the direction subsequent stories will pursue. The future isn't perfect, just improved. People in the 24th century are by and large better than they were in the 20th century, just as in the 20th century people are improved over what they were in the 16th century.

In Trek Classic, Kirk and McCoy, and McCoy and Spock had realistic disagreements. Under stress human tempers would flare and Spock would come close to expressing the Vulcan equivalent of exasperation. On TNG there is no apparent stress—except with people who are not regular members of the crew. Visitors seem to easily rub people the wrong way, as evidenced by Lwaxana Troi.

Riker's encounter with his estranged father a few seasons back is another example. And in season six when Scotty gets on Geordi's nerves, LaForge explodes and tells Montgomery Scott off. This never happens between Riker and Picard, or Picard and anyone in the regular cast. It's a strange schizophrenic approach to the characters on THE NEXT GENERATION, and it can all be traced back to Roddenberry. He made it very clear that the new crew of the Enterprise were "perfect," even though they were only 75 years in advance of the squabbling crew of Trek Classic.

But this seems to be changing now, and rather than demeaning Roddenberry's dream, it is broadening it into a great and more believable reality. After all, if someone is "perfect," then what goals could they have? The future depicted in STAR TREK, whether in Classic Trek or THE NEXT GENERATION is by no means a perfect world. It is an improved future hundreds of years beyond our own, but it is also more complex with just as many difficult problems as we have today.

By showing a humanity which has moved beyond many of the shortcomings of today is admirable, but to proclaim that they have abruptly triumphed over millions of years of emotional strife is unrealistic. Better that we see that they have left some of that strife behind, just as 20th century humanity has in many respects left behind the strife they lived with 300 years before.

Roddenberry wanted to try to use NEXT GENERATION to finish what he had begun in the '60s with the original STAR TREK, but he recognized that not everyone would pick up on this right away, just as it took years for all of the nuances of Classic STAR TREK to be recognized and appreciated.

"I thought several times that the world of drama would have stood up and cheered us," Roddenberry observed near the end of his life, "but no, only silence. But there is one advantage, one thing happening: all of these episodes are brought back and rerun every year. What will happen with STAR TREK—THE NEXT GENERATION is almost identical to what happened to the original STAR TREK as larger and larger audiences become acquainted with the program. The original STAR TREK audience now says, 'Hurrah, what fine shows!' This has brought us considerable pleasure that they would notice it. STAR TREK—THE NEXT GENERATION is on that same path now and more so. The time will come when the second series will attain its true stature. I just hope some of it happens while I am still alive. I'm not jealous that I don't have praise. This happens very broadly in contacts with humans. The world is not necessarily poorer because a painter or playwright is not recognized in his or her lifetime."

CHAPTER 5

COLLISION: CROSSOVERS

by Carlton Martin

It's the STAR TREK crossovers from across time. Spock meets Picard. Geordi meets Scotty. And Sarek meets his maker.

Ever since the inception of STAR TREK: THE NEXT GENERATION, fans of the original STAR TREK wondered what happened to the familiar crew of the Enterprise. True, Kirk, Spock, Bones and the others had experienced more adventures as chronicled in the ongoing STAR TREK film series, but what about the time which passed between the end of STAR TREK and the beginning of THE NEXT GENERATION?

The official chronology asserted that a period of seventy-five years had elapsed between some point (generally given as the events at the conclusion of STAR TREK IV: THE VOYAGE HOME) and the NEXT GENERATION premiere episode "Encounter At Farpoint." This didn't seem to leave much hope for seeing any classic STAR TREK characters on the new show. Except perhaps for Spock, who could easily have lived long enough to see the christening of the Enterprise 1701-D.

But could something like this ever happen? Between William Shatner's strident vocal dismissals of THE NEXT GENERATION, and the as-yet-uncertain future of the fledgling spin-off, it seemed unlikely that there would ever be any sort of linkage between the two eras of Gene Roddenberry's brave new universe.

Old-time STAR TREK aficionados were pleasantly surprised to see DeForest Kelley on hand for the maiden voyage of STAR TREK—THE NEXT GENERATION and its brand-new Enterprise. The appearance of the extremely ancient Leonard

GEORGE
TAKEI AND
NICHELLE
NICHOLS
ON DECEM-
BER 5,
1991 AT
THE HOLLY-
WOOD CAL-
IFORNIA
MANN CHI-
NESE THE-
ATRE STAR
TREK SIG-
NATURE
CEREMO-
NY.

© 1991
Ortega/Galell
a Ltd.

"Bones" McCoy served as the official stamp of approval on the new undertaking. But this crossover appearance was just a cameo. It wasn't very clear whether or not any of the new characters knew exactly who this mumbling old codger really was. McCoy's presence demonstrated that he was still alive, thanks no doubt to medical technology and his general irascibility, but it told us nothing about the character's life during the last seventy-five years.

As the new series groped about for direction, it mentioned the classic STAR TREK only once more: by blatantly stealing from the episode "The Naked Time." McCoy and the old Enterprise were mentioned in the early first-season episode "The Naked Now" (perhaps in an attempt to pass off a swipe as a homage), and McCoy's antidote was eagerly sought, only to prove useless. Perhaps Beverly Crusher's discovery of a new cure was meant to show that the new show could stand on its own. It would stand on its own in time, but this was really a shaky beginning, and "The Naked Now" invited unkind (but perhaps justified) comparisons to the twenty-plus year-old television episode "The Naked Time."

UPDATING THE OLD

Wisely, THE NEXT GENERATION plugged away without any more ill-conceived "homages" until the show's second season, when Dr. Catherine Pulaski, Beverly Crusher's single-season replacement, found herself in the middle of "Unnatural Selection," This time around, they at least had the presence of mind not to refer directly to STAR TREK's original take on an aging-disease story.

"Unnatural Selection" involved a different problem with the same symptoms. But comparison to the original STAR TREK was still unavoidable, not only because the basic threats in the two stories were so painfully similar, but also because the character of Dr. Pulaski was a thinly-veiled attempt to introduce a "Bones" McCoy character into the new series. THE NEXT GENERATION was improving, but not in episodes like "The Naked Now" and "Unnatural Selection," which drew too heavily on the original STAR TREK. THE NEXT GENERATION fared better when relying on its own merits.

Likewise, THE NEXT GENERATION did not feature many of the familiar aliens from STAR TREK. At first, Klingons were the only exception. Although Worf provided a link with the Klingons of the past, he was very much a modern Klingon. In its use of Klingons, THE NEXT GENERATION built an imposing new structure on the foundation of the past, rather than excavating the site and falling in.

Romulans would not fare quite so well in the world of THE NEXT GENERATION. The attempt in "The Neutral Zone," to re-introduce the Romulans as villains (after the Ferengi quickly devolved into comic relief), was anticlimactic. Although THE NEXT GENERATION would make better use of the Romulans in the future, they would never quite cut it as out-and-out villains.

Vulcans were easily the most scarce of the classic STAR TREK aliens as far as THE NEXT GENERATION was concerned. This helped avoid any obvious comparisons to the original series, as did the avoidance of such obvious link-ups as having guest characters who were descendants Kirk or any of the other original Enterprise crew members. (Statistically speaking, it seems more likely that they'd run into descendants of Kirk before they encountered anybody else's grandchildren.)

Beyond Suzie Plakson's single appearance as an incidental Vulcan character in the second season episode "The Schizoid Man," THE NEXT GENERATION made its way to its third season without any direct reference to Vulcans. Suddenly all this changed. Anyone who missed the promotional trailers for the episode in question was undoubtedly surprised when it became obvious that Spock's father Sarek was going to make a guest appearance on THE NEXT GENERATION!

SAREK

Scripted by renowned fantasist Peter S. Beagle and directed by Les Landau, "Sarek" marked the first of Mark Lenard's two highly impressive guest shots on THE NEXT GENERATION. By the time of this story, Sarek has reached the ripe old age of two hundred and two years, and has remarried another Earth woman. He has come on board the Enterprise to lead important negotiations with the Legarans, an elusive people who apparently need steaming mud baths to function off their home world. (Unfortunately, we never get to see what they look like—but then, that's not the point of the story.)

After Sarek and his small entourage board the Enterprise, strange tensions develop among the crew of the ship. At first Picard sees no link between these events and hopes to get to know this great man of his time. The Ambassador and his wife attend a Mozart recital their first night on the ship, but Sarek leaves suddenly in the middle of the performance. Deanna is stunned to see a tear in the venerable Vulcan's eye just before his departure. Soon afterwards, a huge brawl breaks out in Ten Forward, and when Riker tries to break it up he gets belted in the face for his troubles.

Deanna reports her observation of Sarek's tear to Picard, and believes that this is connected to the brawl and other disturbances among the crew. At the recital, she also sensed that Sarek had briefly lost emotional control. Doctor Crusher observes that this might be a symptom of Ben Dai, a disease affecting Vulcans of advanced age.

If this is causing Ambassador Sarek to lose control, then his Vulcan telepathic powers may be transmitting his powerful emotional problem all over the ship and its crew. When confronted with this theory, Sarek's human assistant denies everything. Sarek's wife is also defensive, but Sakkath, Sarek's Vulcan assistant, cannot tell a lie, and finally admits the truth to Data: Sakkath has been using his own telepathic abilities to help Sarek maintain control.

A FINAL TRIUMPH

Sarek is outraged and dismisses Sakkath. He does, however, consent to be tested for Ben Dai syndrome. On the other hand, he will not go along with Picard's desire to postpone the Legaran negotiations until the tests have been completed. Picard's insistence leads Sarek to lose his temper; once the Vulcan calms down, he realizes that Picard is right, and proposes a solution. With a mind meld, Sarek can deposit his own emotional aspects in Picard's mind, while drawing on Picard's strength and balance to carry him through the difficult negotiations.

The negotiations are successful, but they drag on, and Picard must endure the weight of Sarek's regrets, and his long unvoiced love for his first wife Amanda and their son Spock. He endures this ordeal, and the mind-meld is reversed before it does any damage to Picard or Sarek. Sarek retires to Vulcan, his long and distinguished career capped by one final success, while Picard has gotten to know him better than he'd ever dreamed possible.

This was a brilliant merging of elements from two eras of STAR TREK, and one which went far beyond mere nostalgia. In positing the existence of a disease which unleashes the long-suppressed emotions of Vulcans, this episode actually added a crucial piece to the puzzle of the Vulcan psyche, which apparently is not based on as firm a foundation as was previously thought.

UNIFICATION: TWO TREKS IN ONE!

Despite the hype surrounding it, and the many disappointments to be found in the show as filmed, the two-episode story of "Unification" still stands as the central crossover between the classic STAR TREK and THE NEXT GENERATION. The set-up for the first half is simple but effective, a teaser that draws us into the story. The script was by Jeri Taylor, from a story by Rick Berman and Michael Piller; the director was Les Landau.

The Enterprise is called to a nearby Starbase, where Captain Picard is summoned to a secret meeting with Fleet Admiral Brackett. Brackett informs Picard of the Federation's concerns: it seems that a high-ranking ambassador has disappeared, only to turn up on the Romulan home world, Romulus. A blurred image gathered by intelligence reveals the identity of the person in question: Spock. Brackett assigns Picard to investigate this possible defection.

Picard takes the Enterprise to the planet Vulcan, where he hopes that Sarek can shed some light on his son's actions and motivations. Picard beams down and sends Riker and the ship to investigate a crashed Ferengi vessel. This seems to have some relevance to the question at hand when Geordi discovers traces of a Vulcan alloy in the Ferengi wreck.

Picard finds that Sarek's wife Perrin has some reservations about Picard's visit. Sarek is gravely ill, dying of Ben Dai Syndrome. Spock did not visit his father before his departure, so it seems unlikely that Sarek will be able to assist Picard in any way. But in light of the mind meld between Sarek and Picard, Perrin allows Picard to visit her husband.

AS THE END DRAWS NEAR

Sarek is dying, and his emotions periodically overpower him. Picard tells him that Spock has vanished. Suddenly, Sarek recognizes Picard, and expresses shock at the news that Spock is on Romulus. He reveals that Spock is acquainted with a Romulan senator named Pardek. Spock has been calling for an open dialogue with the Romulans, a plea that has fallen on deaf ears on both sides.

The notion that Spock has defected is utterly impossible as far as Sarek is concerned. After making this observation, Sarek's thoughts lose their focus, and he begins to ramble on about Spock's childhood, and his inability to obey Sarek. Then lucidity returns for a moment, and he gives his friend a message for his son. "Tell him, Picard. . . live long and. . . "

". . . prosper," Picard whispers, completing Sarek's thought.

Picard returns to the Enterprise and heads for the Klingon homeworld, where he hopes to meet with Gowron, the Klingon leader who owes Picard and Worf more than a few favors. Gowron initially ignores Picard's transmissions, for it seems he is busy rewriting history, and the Federation's part in Gowron's rise to power has no place in official Klingon lore.

Examining the evidence from the Federation, Picard determines that Spock has met with Pardek, who is considered a radical among the Romulans due to his philosophy of peaceful co-existence.

The Klingons finally reply, but claim that Gowron is too busy with affairs of state to spare any time for Picard. Picard politely demands a cloaked vessel, but says that he will understand if Gowron will not provide it. Gowron quickly changes his mind and hands over a ship and crew for Picard's use. Data and

Picard begin to prepare for their secret mission, and are carefully disguised as Romulans.

THE MYSTERIOUS MISSION

Geordi determines that the metal parts from the Ferengi wreck are from a Vulcan deflector assembly. Moreover, they are from a decommissioned Vulcan ship, the T'Pau. (This is a nice reference to "Amok Time," and the Vulcan matriarch of that name.) According to official records, the T'Pau is in storage at Qualtor Two, a space junkyard.

Data and Picard, now looking like Romulans, board the Klingon ship, which is under the command of Captain K'Vada. K'Vada has a typical Klingon distaste for covert operations, and is none too thrilled about going to the Romulan home world, either. He guesses that their mission involves the search for Spock (what, again?), but Picard denies it.

Meanwhile, the Enterprise travels to Qualtor Two, hoping to discover how fragments of the T'Pau wound up in the wreckage of a Ferengi freighter. Klim Dokachin, the manager of the junkyard, is reluctant to help, but does so anyway. The T'Pau is indeed missing. Another vessel, the Tripoli, also proves to be missing from its docking site— but supplies have been routed to that vessel on a regular basis for quite some time now.

A shipment is scheduled that very day. The Enterprise darkens its exterior illumination and conceals itself among the other derelict ships. Riker is certain that another ship will show up to intercept the supplies that will be beamed to the empty site of the Tripoli. And he is correct. Another spaceship drops out of warp and assumes the Tripoli's docking site. But when Riker hails this ship, it fires on the Enterprise, whose return fire causes the mystery vessel to explode.

ONWARD TO ROMULUS

Meanwhile, en route to Romulus on the cloaked Klingon ship, Picard receives the news that Ambassador Sarek has died. When they finally arrive at Romulus, Data and Picard prepare to beam down. Picard muses that he now has an additional task to perform: he must tell Spock of Sarek's demise. He hopes that he will be able to accomplish this part of his mission; Sarek and Spock had never fully reconciled their differences over the long years of their relationship.

Picard and Data beam down to the Romulan street where Spock was secretly photographed. Someone is obviously watching them from the moment they arrive. Data and Picard see Pardek and attempt to follow him, but armed Romulans stop them at gunpoint and take them to a secret cave where Pardek awaits them. Picard explains that he is searching for Spock. At this point, Spock steps out from behind a wall and announces that Picard has found the one he is seeking.

"Unification I" is an exciting and compelling quest story combined with a bit of mystery. But now that Spock had finally shown himself, would THE NEXT GENERATION carry the ball or fumble?

UNIFICATION II: SPOCK SURVIVES

The story resumes in the second half of "Unification." This is where much of the disappointment surrounding Spock's appearance originates: after all the big build-up, his presence winds up being anticlimactic. "Unification II" turns out to be a talky, meandering episode in which the activities of Riker and the crew are far more interesting than the scenes involving Spock, Data and Picard.

Spock serves more as an icon than as a character in "Unification II," and it seems reasonable to assume that the writers for this episode were so overwhelmed by the presence of such an imposing icon that they really didn't know what to do with the character, treating him with kid gloves and sparing him any real dramatic development or interaction. They did a lot better by Sarek: Mark Lenard's portrayal of the dying ambassador is the real dramatic highlight of "Unification," and one of the most memorable acting jobs to be found anywhere in the entire body of STAR TREK, old and new. "Unification I" was a strong lead-in, but "Unification II" was largely a let-down, and the scenes in which Riker and the Enterprise crew track the missing ship were far more engaging than any scenes involving Spock.

Even so, "Unification II," scripted by Michael Piller from a story by Piller and NEXT GENERATION producer Rick Berman, serves as the crucial link between classic TREK and THE NEXT GENERATION. The episode was directed by Cliff Bole.

THE UNDISCOVERED COUNTRY

"Unification" was clearly intended as a lead-in for that year's theatrical release, STAR TREK VI: THE UNDISCOVERED COUNTRY. Spock's obscure references to the events of that film were certainly tantalizing. After the broadcast of "Unification," many rumors circulated regarding the then-forthcoming film. One suggested that the story would end with Spock's wedding, an occasion mentioned in THE NEXT GENERATION's third-season classic episode "Sarek." This would, of course, necessitate the presence of a young Lieutenant Jean-Luc Picard at the end of the film.

The trailers for the film fostered the impression that the movie involved a romance for Spock. But it turned out that what appeared to be a passionate embrace with Kim Catrall, turned out to be the mind-meld that reveals Catrall's character as the traitor. There was no romance for Spock in THE UNDISCOVERED COUNTRY. The details of Spock's wedding remain a mystery, and no wife, dead or living, is mentioned anywhere in either part of "Unification."

There was, however, one crossover with THE NEXT GENERATION in THE UNDISCOVERED COUNTRY. The Klingon lawyer (Klingons have lawyers?) assigned the unhappy task of defending Kirk and McCoy was named Worf, and was played by Michael Dorn— the character was the direct ancestor of the Worf portrayed by Dorn in THE NEXT GENERATION. And the final action packed scenes of the movie took place on the planet Khitomer, future site of the Romulan attack that would lead to Worf being raised by humans.

TO SPOCK OR NOT TO SPOCK

Thoughts of Spock rose briefly the following year. When the sixth-season episode "Face of the Enemy" was in the works, NEXT GENERATION writer Michael Piller jokingly suggested that one of the Romulan dignitaries in suspended animation in that episode might actually turn out to be Spock. To top off the joke, he proposed having one of the frozen Romulans say something, upon defrosting, to the effect that Spock had been killed along the way. Apparently this joke did not provoke too much laughter, and Spock is, as far as we know, still alive and kicking on the planet Romulus.

With the ratings success of "Unification," it seemed that it would only be a matter of time before another member of the original Enterprise crew showed up on TNG. And in the sixth season of the series, one of them did just that.

THE RESURRECTION OF SCOTTY

It was with mixed feelings that many heard the news that Scotty would soon be appearing on THE NEXT GENERATION. Some couldn't help but joke: "They find Scotty drifting in space— and throw him back!" Between the disappointment many felt after "Unification," another crossover seemed a dubious proposition at best.

It turned out to be a fun episode that revealed, among other things, Scotty's greatest secret. Ronald D. Moore, a real classic TREK aficionado, was assigned to script this outing, and Alexander Singer would direct.

The basic notion that made "Relics" possible had nothing to do with Scotty. In fact, the script that inspired it was a freelance submission that was almost entirely discarded. All that was retained by THE NEXT GENERATION's producers was a simple technical idea that made Scotty's return dramatically feasible. Other classic Trek characters were considered, but Scotty, as one of the most popular characters outside of the Big Three, was ultimately chosen.

In "Relics," the Enterprise-D discovers something long theorized but never before encountered: a Dyson sphere. This is a construct built around a star so that civilizations can live on the inside of the sphere, taking advantage of natural solar energy in an area vastly larger than the surface of a single planet. This discovery occurs because the Enterprise has detected an old Federation distress signal. Upon arrival at the impossibly huge artifact, they discover a small spacecraft that appears to have been wrecked on the outer surface of the Dyson sphere some seventy-five years earlier.

Geordi and an Away Team investigate and find no one alive on board— and no corpses. But Geordi is intrigued to discover that the Transporters are still functioning, although at a low power level. He discovers that someone had apparently set up a closed loop in the Transporter mechanism. Two signals are locked in. One has deteriorated too much to be retrieved, but the other is almost one hundred percent. An amazed LaForge brings back Montgomery Scott, who has been cycling through a Transporter field for three quarters of a century!

BETWEEN PRESENT AND PAST

The "serious" part of this episode involves one relic, the Dyson sphere. When the Enterprise enters the sphere to examine it, they discover that it has been abandoned for centuries, if not millennia. Matters get complicated when they try to leave.

The other relic, of course, is Scotty himself. Gregarious as ever, he tries to fit in, but soon finds that there's not that much for him to do on this new Enterprise. There's a fine comedic interplay between James Doohan and LeVar Burton as, time and again, Scotty tries to help out but only manages to get in Geordi's way.

Geordi, after all, is one of the nicest guys in the galaxy, and he doesn't want to offend anyone, but he is hard pressed to keep his exasperation concealed. Scotty finally realizes the situation and becomes fairly despondent. At one point, he recreates the bridge of the original starship Enterprise for a nostalgic, alcohol-tinged visit, where he is joined by Captain Picard.

This was not as easy to do as it appears in the episode as filmed. Rebuilding an entire replica of the sixties-style Enterprise bridge was simply impossible under budgetary restrictions (creating a Dyson sphere on film wasn't exactly cheap in itself). In fact, the idea was completely canned at one point— producer Rick Berman basically said to forget it. And Moore's original idea of having Scotty interact with Holodeck images of Kirk and the others was also deemed much too expensive, although not impossible; they could have used clips from old shows. After some thought, the idea of the empty bridge, which was actually more poignant than the other notion, was revived.

Ultimately, the story develops in such a way that the Enterprise is in danger once again, unable to slip past the defenses of the Dyson sphere. This might be a bit predictable. Geordi can't save the day on his own, and he needs Scotty's help. Scotty reveals what many have suspected all along when he admonishes Geordi to stop giving Captain Picard honest and accurate estimates of how long a job will take— Scotty has always multiplied his estimates, in order to make himself look like a real miracle worker! Of course everything works out, Scotty feels needed, and soon he's on his way again, after a seventy-five-year delay. But retirement is out of the question. There's too much now to learn and discover in this new age.

Thanks to James Doohan, Scotty comes across as charming, humorous and much better served than he's been in more recent STAR TREK movies. He doesn't bang his head on a bulkhead even once! In fact, "Relics" might do better by Scotty than any episode of the original series did.

KLINGON MESSIAH

The most recent crossover between the classic STAR TREK and THE NEXT GENERATION may have slipped by many viewers. It occurs in the sixth-season episode "Rightful Heir," in which the legendary Klingon hero Kahless, portrayed by Kevin Conway, appears to return to life and make a claim on the entire Klingon Empire.

The third-season STAR TREK episode "The Savage Curtain" featured the same character, played by Robert Herron. The contrast between the two takes on this character also provides an interesting contrast between the general outlooks of STAR TREK classic and THE NEXT GENERATION.

For starters, it seems unlikely that any NEXT GENERATION episode would begin with the discovery of Abraham Lincoln floating in space! (Then again, episodes like "Q-Pid," with its Robin Hood theme, and the occasional forays into hard-boiled detective fiction and Sherlock Holmes, might cause one to reconsider this.) To be perfectly honest, "The Savage Curtain" was far from being one of STAR TREK's greatest moments, although it's still a great deal more watchable than "Spock's Brain."

Lincoln, of course, was a projection created by a rock creature keen on examining humanoid conceptions of good and evil. Rehashing the basic territory of "Arena," this creature wanted to know if good was better than evil, or vice versa, and apparently felt that physical combat was the best way to find out. Kirk was teamed up with Lincoln to combat two historical characters who represented evil: Earth's own murderous Colonel Green, and the thoroughly vicious Klingon warrior Kahless. Robert Herron made Kahless a truly nasty bad guy, easily the most unpleasant Klingon ever to grace the series.

"Rightful Heir" revived the same character, but with a totally different twist. In all fairness, perhaps the entity in "The Savage Curtain" recreated Kahless from the human conception of him—but here, seen from the perspective of THE NEXT GENERATION, Kahless is anything but an evil character. And he is viewed, quite clearly, as a part of Klingon culture, rather than a stereotyped villain.

AN HISTORIC RECREATION

In "Rightful Heir," Kahless is first encountered by Worf when he goes to a Klingon monastery. Kahless appears to Worf while Worf is involved in yet another Klingon religious ritual. At first this seems to be a spiritual visitation, and the monks make much of it, but soon enough Kahless appears in the flesh, back after millennia and ready to fix up the Klingon Empire.

Gowron, the current ruler, is not pleased with this, and is less than thrilled when Worf, once one of his supporters, seems prepared to side with Kahless and the monks. Kahless himself is a dynamic character, confident enough to endure various tests to assure his authenticity. Worf is torn between the charisma of this legend-made-flesh and the dictates of logic.

In an intriguing plot twist, Kahless turns out to be both the real thing and a fraud: the monks, hoping to quell the troubles of the Klingon Empire, actually cloned Kahless from the DNA in an ancient bloodstain. Kahless-2 is pathetically unaware of all this. As far as he knows, he is the one to reunite the Klingon Empire, simply because he's the one who put it together in the first place!

Comparing the Kahless of STAR TREK's "The Savage Curtain" and THE NEXT GENERATION's "Rightful Heir" shows up the basic differences between the two shows. THE NEXT GENERATION clearly examines alien cultures in greater depth. The Klingons are warlike and aggressive but they are also honorable (admittedly something seen as far back as "Day Of The Dove"), not just arbitrary stand-ins for evil. THE NEXT GENERATION has built on the foundation of STAR TREK most admirably in its ongoing treatment of Klingons.

ROMULANS REDUX

THE NEXT GENERATION did not fare so well in the case of the Romulans. Their return at the end of the first season ("The Neutral Zone") was dismally anticlimactic: they showed up and acted like they were thinking about doing something unpleasant, but didn't really do anything at all.

Later on, the character of Sela failed to create a new Romulan arch-enemy and she has vanished from sight after her tough-gal posturings in "Unification II." In the stories leading up to "Unification" Romulans were used fairly effectively as standard-issue heavies (setting aside the Sela question), but once "Unification" was over they had lost that edge.

FORWARD— INTO THE PAST?

The general consensus at this point is that the seventh season of THE NEXT GENERATION will be its last. The seventh season is scheduled to go into production a month early so that cast and crew will be free to begin work on the first NEXT GENERATION movie in April of 1994. And although no script has yet been chosen, two are in the works. Either one would, if filmed, involve at least some of the classic STAR TREK characters.

Rick Berman, tapped by Paramount to keep the Enterprise flying into movie theaters on a projected bi-annual basis, arranged for two scripts to be worked up for consideration. So far, neither one has reached its final form, much less been chosen, but here's how they break down at present:

Ronald D. Moore (scripter of "Relics") and Brannon Braga are working on a NEXT GENERATION story that will, it is rumored, send Picard's Enterprise back into time for an encounter with Kirk and his crew, opening the opportunity for any of a number of the original cast to appear in the tale.

(Both Leonard Nimoy and William Shatner seem to have approved this notion— provided that the shooting script— and wages— meet with their approval.)

DUAL FUTURES

The other possible NEXT GENERATION feature treatment in the works is by Maurice Hurley, best remembered as THE NEXT GENERATION's executive producer for the show's first two seasons. Originally, Hurley had no plans to use any of the classic STAR TREK characters in his story, but was swayed by a suggestion from a friend of his— an actor named William Shatner.

No one is releasing any details about the plots of either of these scripts. However, Rick Berman makes it clear that the story of the first NEXT GENERATION movie will focus primarily on the crew of the Enterprise 1701-D. Any crossover with Kirk, Spock and the other STAR TREK characters will be part of the story, but not the whole story.

To date, Rick Berman and Paramount have looked at the two ideas in progress, with plenty of input from Berman, but they have not chosen one over the other. It is much too early to speculate about the movie, its plot, or exactly how the old crew members will be involved, if at all. But it is intriguing that both versions resort to time travel for their crossovers.

So far, television's NEXT GENERATION has stayed away from using time travel in its crossover episodes, relying on a projected increase in human life span to bring McCoy on board, taking advantage of the natural longevity of Vulcans for the episodes involving Sarek and Spock, and creating a unique way of bringing back Scotty.

The time travel angle brings up memories of the classic "Yesterday's Enterprise" (and its woeful sequel, as personified by Tasha Yar's Romulan daughter!). Perhaps the movie could be titled "The Day Before Yesterday's Enterprise."

All levity aside, the Moore/Braga concept could serve to provide one final, all-encompassing crossover. After all, it would be a bit on the tedious side if THE NEXT GENERATION felt obliged to come up with new and different ways to involve every old character in future episodes or motion pictures.

One thing, however, is certain: any crossover between the two generations of STAR TREK in the first NEXT GENERATION film is going to be well thought out, and well executed, as the concept is one that Rick Berman and his creative team will give plenty of thought to before they commit it to celluloid. Whatever happens, it will undoubtedly by spectacular, and well worth the wait!

CHAPTER 6

THE CONTINUING VOYAGES: CONCLUSIONS

By Dennis K. Fischer

What more can be said about these two shows? How about a wrap-up in which we look back over what has been explored and see if a definitive decision can be reached in our photo-finish.

While many had their misgivings, I actively looked forward to the 1987 premiere of STAR TREK: THE NEXT GENERATION. So what if it wasn't further adventures of Kirk, Spock, McCoy et al., the movies were still doing an adequately entertaining job.

By being syndicated, there was less worry about the network censors and other hindrances. Plus Paramount, a studio that had long undervalued STAR TREK until it discovered a vast underground of merchandising at STAR TREK conventions, was actually going to pony up about $1 million an episode to see that it was done right.

In retrospect, the first year of NEXT GENERATION must be regarded as something of a shakedown cruise, with the series reaching its highest potential in the third and fourth seasons. At its best, NEXT GENERATION displayed fine acting, powerful storytelling and production values which rank it among the very best of '80s and '90s, television.

Being daring goes back to the original TREK CLASSIC where Gene Roddenberry, in his pilot, makes reference to Hell being a fairy tale learned in childhood and perceptively warned of the dangers of a culture amusing itself to death. STAR TREK is still

GENE ROD-
DENBERY

MAJEL BARRETT RODDENBERRY

© 1992
Ortega/Galell
a Ltd.

noted as having the first inter-racial kiss on television, albeit in one of its worst episodes ("Plato's Stepchildren").

STAR TREK performed little morality plays in science fiction guise to bring a secular humanist viewpoint into homes across America and the world. Many people have responded very positively to this viewpoint. Some have even made a quasi-religion out of it.

ACTION VS. INTELLECT

The emphasis in the '60s was on action and adventure. The hero of the story typically would be called on to indulge in fisticuffs to fight his way out of a problem, but we knew he was being motivated by good and true purposes.

In '60s television, the hero, in this case James T. Kirk, was expected to resort to some action which would resolve the conflict set up in the show. All moral dilemmas were expected to have solutions. This gave Trek Classic a nice combination of dramatic dialogue and engaging action with clear-cut heroes to root for.

By the late '80's such an approach was felt to be hopelessly out of date. In real life most problems are resolved via negotiation, and worse yet, some seem genuinely insoluble. Additionally, Gene Roddenberry wanted to get away from a dictatorial leader who dominated the action the way Kirk did. He wanted to portray a future which was open to many different viewpoints.

HARMONY VS. DISHARMONY

This gained a more intelligent approach to the conflicts arising on the show. However, since the essence of drama is conflict, the confrontation seemed to be less extreme and dramatic. It was a more cerebral but less emotionally satisfying way of dealing with difficulties. This aspect alienated the more action-oriented fans of Trek Classic while winning some new converts who felt the older approach was far too simplistic and violence oriented.

Another change was to be the lack of conflict among crew members of the Enterprise (a dictum which has since been softened). One of the delights that slowly grew out of the original series was the lighthearted "insult/debates" between Spock and McCoy. They represented the intellectual and emotional sides of Kirk's nature, each arguing for preeminence. The pair, who obviously respected each other, would verbally spar with one another almost constantly, displaying their wit and trying to get the upper hand. The routine would steal every scene.

NEXT GENERATION wanted to depict an ideal humanity, however, in which such insult fests were a thing of the past. They later recanted this dictum slightly by having Dr. Pulaski initially dislike Data in the second season, taking on some of the crustiness of a McCoy. This approach proved short-lived. Writers for THE NEXT GENERATION complained that this chumminess among the crew members made it difficult to generate conflicts which would facilitate drama. But it also forced them to become more inventive and find other targets for conflict outside the core cast of central characters.

COMMERCIAL CONSIDERATION

Another difference between Trek Classic and NEXT GENERATION simply has to do with the breakdown of time. Back in the '60s, the FCC, working for once on behalf of the American public, insisted that television networks could include no more than 8 minutes of commercials per hour, which meant that the average STAR TREK episode ran 52 minutes (which also accounts for why scenes were continually being clipped away when the series started syndication and why they have been artificially sped-up using special equipment in some of the more recent incarnations).

NEXT GENERATION is produced when the time allowed for commercials has almost doubled, which means apart from credits and coming attractions, the average NEXT GENERATION episode only runs 42 minutes. There is almost 15% more time for a story to develop to a resolution on Trek Classic than there is for NEXT GENERATION.

Additionally, the format for STAR TREK had a teaser (a short scene or scenes to set the stage) plus four acts. Each act except the last one had a climax to keep the viewer hooked through the commercial break. NEXT GENERATION was formatted with a teaser and five acts. This is more awkward and necessitates an additional climax be inserted, often just a few minutes after a previous one.

DUELING PLOTLINES

Additionally, when NEXT GENERATION premiered, the first season was rife with A plot/B plot stories. It is not uncommon for a multi-charactered show to have subplots. Unfortunately, the two plots on NEXT GENERATION usually weren't related dramatically or thematically. In fact, often one plot was simply a ticking clock device, which means that some scientific technicality needed to be resolved by a proscribed time to ensure the safety of the ship.

There were times when a plot which could have used more time to develop the characters or conflicts would be sacrificed for an uninteresting and artificial B plot. During its first season, THE NEXT GENERATION did make the daring move of killing off Lt. Tasha Yar (reportedly because Denise Crosby was bored with the part). However, even there TV GUIDE spoiled the surprise and her death seemed thrown away at the beginning of "Skin of Evil".

One big mistake which NEXT GENERATION initially made was its insistence that each character have a featured moment in every episode. Roddenberry felt that William Shatner's ego began to dominate STAR TREK in a way he hadn't intended. While he believed in leadership, he didn't want any one cast member pushed forward to the exclusion of the others.

As a consequence, valuable screen time was sometimes taken up with trivialities to allow each character to get his or her featured spot. Even so, the first season seemed to have no idea what to do with Geordi LaForge or Deanna Troi, and some of its ideas for Wesley Crusher and William Riker were simply wrongheaded. Fortunately, Roddenberry was an excellent judge of acting talent and each cast member was able to shine when called upon to do so. There was enough material to go around.

COMMAND DECISIONS

Splitting the command between Picard (the man of thought) and Riker (the man of action) presented an interesting dramatic problem, but one that presented no real difficulties for the audience. David Gerrold, writing in THE WORLD OF STAR TREK, had pointed out that it was unnecessarily risky for the captain of a ship to beam down to every dangerous and unknown territory. Roddenberry took up this idea by initially keeping Picard aboard the ship and having Riker lead all the Away Teams. It was presumed that Jonathan Frakes would be an object of lust. Who knew that a few years later, Patrick Stewart would be declared the sexiest man on television. This is a source of endless amusement and bemusement to Mr. Stewart, who is only too cognizant of the reactions of women when he was younger and first lost his hair.

When the show first aired, many viewers kept looking for a correspondence between Trek Classic and NEXT GENERATION characters, as if Roddenberry had some magic formula for success and would simply plug it into the new situation. Fortunately Roddenberry was smarter than that, but even so it took some time for the characters to become real personalities.

Apart from the Trek triumvirate of Kirk, Spock and McCoy, most of the other characters were only given stereotyped caricatures to perform. Scotty was the hard-drinking, hard-working Scottish engineer who'd rather spend time with his machines than people. Uhura was the comely communications officer, often little more than a telephone operator in outer space, while Sulu, occasionally noted for being overly enthusiastic about his hobbies, was simply the requisite "bus driver." Late addition Chekov was supposed to be a Kirk-in-training with a Beatle wig to appeal to the younger generation.

While a few early episodes had Picard making bad decisions, surrendering too quickly or even giving up the ship, the captain quickly settled into being an ideal commander, commanding loyalty and respect from those who served under him. Early episodes hinted at an unacknowledged and perhaps guilty romance between Beverly Crusher and Picard, but later they just seem to be old friends.

COMPARING THE CAPTAINS

Kirk could make bad decisions too, most notably keeping the arms race going in "Private Little War" He had liaisons with attractive women on a highly frequent basis, but for the most part he was devoted to his ship. The rule of thumb seemed to be "out of sight, out of mind." Kirk and Picard share an interest in finding out about aliens, though in STAR TREK V, Kirk simply wants to kill one for pretending to be "God" while Picard frequently fails to ask questions of some of the more interesting aliens he encounters.

Both are basically moral, principled men, though Kirk is more likely to rush in where angels fear to tread to resolve some sticky issue. (He took the Prime Directive, i.e. don't interfere with alien cultures, a lot less seriously than Picard, who would sometimes rather see a bad situation continue to its logical conclusion than attempt to better things.)

Picard has received some of the best exploration of character shows on NEXT GENERATION. Particularly strong are his sense of being haunted by his experience with the Borg, who took over his body and controlled him for a time. Additionally, we see that he has a rocky relationship with his brother, who stayed at home to tend the family grapes while Jean-Luc reaped renown as a Starfleet commander.

In one notable episode, "Inner Light," he got to experience life as it would have been on another planet had he not been a starship captain (he has the family he didn't allow himself as captain and finds satisfaction in playing the flute). In another he gets to relive a key moment in his life to see what the alternative would have been, discovering that if he had taken the safer route he once regretted not having taken, it would have become a habit that would have prevented him from achieving his present greatness. As a consequence of such episodes, Picard is the most fleshed out of the NEXT GENERATION characters.

EXAMINING SUPPORTING ROSTERS

Riker seemed meant to embody the virile aspects of Kirk. In the early episodes he was the embodiment of the virtues of mankind—strong yet tolerant, intelligent and compassionate, willing to learn from his enemies as well as his friends. He was seen as having no sexual hang-ups, and although it was clear he had once been Deanna Troi's lover, this in no way adversely affected their continuing working relationship and friendship.

The first season made the mistake of having Riker pose too stiffly. Additionally, while Jonathan Frakes has an excellent sense of humor, this was not effectively employed until later seasons, making the character seem to take himself and everything else a tad too seriously. The character looks better in his short, trim beard which he has retained since the second season.

While Riker has been offered a command, he prefers to serve under Picard. We know Riker likes to play the sax and have sex, not necessarily in that order. In fact this aspect of Riker's character was used against him in "The Game" when an alien female pose as a comfort woman and seduced Riker into bringing a seemingly harmless game back to the Enterprise; a game which was actually a mind altering device.

Deanna Troi was called the ship's counselor but didn't do any counseling until the later episodes. Much was made of her ability as an empath, being able to sense emotions in alien races. However, what she sensed was usually something that was obvious to the audience anyway, making her one of the most consistently boring of the crew until her character received some fine-tuning. Additionally she was initially dressed in what looked like a McDonald's waitress outfit, giving way to a Cosmic Cheerleader outfit. Not that I have anything against cleavage, but her uniform stood out among the others for its differences, which were only amended later. There was no real reason for her being on the bridge except to give the men in the audience something to ogle.

THE KLINGON WAY

Worf, as the more alien of the aliens in the main crew, began to dominate as more stories turned on his differences with the other crew members. Initially he could predictably be counted on to advise "attack," which almost never seemed to be taken seriously as an option if he did so. In most respects, Worf simply isn't different enough. He seems like an overly aggressive human most of the time rather than someone really alien. Curiously, the episode "Family" had Worf raised by Russian-Jewish parents, and yet there has never been before or since the slightest hint that Worf has been influenced by his adoptive parents' culture. (Not that he had to offer matzoh balls and chicken soup to someone who was sick, but surely something of his parents should have been incorporated into his character.)

It broke a minor taboo about TV heroes when Worf refused to donate his blood to save a dying Romulan, which gave that particular episode a little edge, but the character's racism is rarely explored. More disturbing to me, after being acclimated to the peaceful ideals of Starfleet Academy and serving the Federation for so long, why does he find the concept of peaceful Klingons so abhorrent when he encounters them in "Birthright"? Here he becomes a proponent of preserving even the negative aspects of his culture rather than redefining what a warrior is. Couldn't he conceive of a warrior being someone who struggles for justice rather than someone who kills enemies and gives the blood cry? Haven't his experiences in Starfleet influenced his outlook in any way?

Dr. Beverly Crusher isn't another "Bones" McCoy, although both are more than competent doctors who care about people. We know she likes dance and worries about her son. She can be forceful or can cozen when it's appropriate, possessing a temper tempered with a real ability to read people. As such, she is one of the most human people on the show but is usually relegated to working in sickbay or underscoring some personal relationship with either Picard or her son, Wesley. Her best episode remains "The Host" where she falls in love with Odan, but can't deal with the parasite's changing of hosts, especially into a new female body.

THE WESLEY SITUATION

No character seemed to provoke more fan resentment than Wesley Crusher. Wesley happened to be Gene Roddenberry's middle name and it's obvious that Wesley is meant to embody the science fictional dreams of Roddenberry's younger self—a bright lad who gets to have exciting adventures alongside adults, and who continually proves his worth. But too many of the early episodes relied on Wesley to save the ship. Roddenberry's intent was to show that there was no age prejudice in the future. However, it seemed to most people that Wesley had been promoted to the bridge over older, more qualified people, and he was something of a smartass besides.

Wesley was never portrayed as a normal teenage boy with normal teenage problems. He didn't hang out with other teenagers, or indulge in many of the activities that teens typically do. Instead he was the type who always did his homework, was respectful to his mother and was simply brilliant. His unintentional Achilles heel is that the character was allowed to brag too much, is too smart for his own good, never seemed to know enough to get away from the bridge when Picard told him to, and began to grate on some of the audience's nerves.

Compare that to Classic Trek's Mr. Spock. His Achilles' Heel was his emotions, which he represses (something that many troubled people would love to be able to do) and can't deal with as successfully (supposedly) as we humans. However, Mr. Spock was an adult who could engineer better than Scotty, could accurately calculate odds in an instant, knew one bit of useful trivia after another, and was basically superior to humans on an almost superhuman level.

If Spock had been played by a teen actor, he too would have been intolerable. He'd paid his dues and used his smarts to good effect. (Isaac Asimov once wrote an article on how intelligence was sexy based on the appeal of Mr. Spock.) A teenager is someone who is just coming to grips with the world, while a Mr. Know-It-All should be someone who believably has mastered it.

Fortunately, Wil Wheaton decided that his real life was more important than his "reel" life and quit the series to seriously pursue his college education. Wesley seemed to throw the show off and now only appears as a sometime guest star the way Q and Lwaxana Troi do. He came back one time to save the ship from mind-numbing games in a bad episode ("The Game") and was actually allowed to screw-up and decide where his loyalties lay at Starfleet Academy in a good one ("The First Duty").

LEONARD
NIMOY ON
NOVEMBER
14, 1992
AS HE
ARRIVES
AT HEMS-
LEY
PALACE
HOTEL FOR
"NIGHT OF
100
STARS"
BENEFIT-
ING THE
ACTORS
FUND OF
AMERICA.

© 1982 Ron
Galella Ltd.

GEORDI AND FRIEND

Geordi LaForge initially floundered as helmsman, the idea being that it was somehow wryly amusing that a blind man was steering the Enterprise. After the first season, one still had no sense of his character. Where there had been a couple of attempts at establishing an engineer, it was only when Geordi was switched to engineering that he began to have any flare, as well as be a character the others would regularly consult. The banana clip visor on his face and his child-like reactions and attitudes didn't help at first. Plus, he seemed more awkward with women than Wesley did, a slightly endearing trait.

LeVar Burton's strength came to the fore slowly as writers began to get a handle on Geordi. His interactions with Starfleet screwup Barclay helped throw his personality into relief. He is obviously good at his job and gets impatient with incompetence, but is also willing to give people a chance or two when prodded. He seems excited by the technobabble he's called upon to recite, and his use of the Holedeck to create simulations to explore his engineering ideas is one of the few really intelligent uses of that extraordinary device.

Data quickly became a focus for many of the writers, apparently looking for a Spock replacement. Actually Data owes more to QUESTOR TAPES, a pilot about an android looking for his creator that Roddenberry wrote and shot in the '70s. Data seems to have or not have emotions as the script calls for it, so as a semi-mechanical man, he's not the least bit consistent.

Brent Spiner is a delight in the role. His talent for mimicry gives the show some added humor while his existential quest for human understanding has led to some of the finer episodes. Now that Data is able to have dreams (as shown in "Birthright"), who knows what changes may be wrought in his character.

THE CHANGING FUTURE

Outside the exemplary crew of the Enterprise, the competence of the rest of Starfleet and the Federation has to be continually called into question, with the definite exception of Sarek. In one of the most powerful NEXT GENERATION episodes, he goes senile. (One must credit the NEXT GENERA-TION with being willing to be unsettling when it is clearly called for, though Trek Classic episodes such as "City On The Edge of Forever," which doesn't have a typically upbeat ending, shows that it was no slouch in that department either.)

In "The Trouble With Tribbles," Kirk claims never to have doubted the intelligence of a Federation representative until then, but somehow that kind of conflict has set the pattern for future encounters. The irritable ambassador in "Metamorphosis" was at least partially explained by her being seriously ill, though the one in "The Deadly Years" simply seems to have an inflated opinion of his abilities. However, NEXT GENERATION has presented such a line-up of Federation yotzes, one wonders how it has survived them all.

Both series have done excellent crazed starship captain episodes. There's Matt Decker (William Windom) in "The Doomsday Machine" and Ben Maxwell (Bob Gunton) in "The Wounded," both of which are well motivated for their extreme responses, and the relative excellence of each story excuses them.

However, consider the annoying Selay and Andican delegates in "Lonely Among Us," Admiral Mark Jameson in "Too Short A Season," the interrogations of Admiral Quinn and Lt. Commander Remmick in "Coming Of Age," the treacherous Starfleet officers in "Conspiracy," and Commander Bruce Maddox who is gung-ho to disassemble Data in "The Measure of a Man."

Then there's William Riker's unpleasant father Kyle Riker, a "legend in the annals of Starfleet" in "The Icarus Factor," the inept dignitaries in "Manhunt," the short-sighted and obnoxious Dr. Paul Stubbs in "Evolution," the sleazy Devonian Rai in "The Price," and the maliciously manipulative Admiral Satie in "The Drumhead." With personnel like these, is Federation dominance of the galaxy such a good thing? Fortunately the principles motivating the Federation are higher than most of the people carrying them out, which can also be said of most countries when it comes to their ethics.

THE NEW ENEMIES

Naturally, the surrounding STAR TREK universe has changed as it came under the guidance of new hands. Originally the Romulans were an honorable race while the Klingons were depicted as treacherous and bloodthirsty. On NEXT GENERATION, the Romulans have been given new headpieces to emphasize alienness just as the movies altered the Klingons (the bumps on the head being caused, perhaps, by having their spinal cords raised from the Federation kicking their butt so many times). The Klingons are now depicted as being particularly deceptive and dishonorable, while we frequently hear Worf extolling the Klingon concepts of honor.

With the Klingons safely (?) at peace with the Federation, it was felt that a new menace should be created. Hints of the "dreaded" Ferengi were dropped in the pilot episode. Originally Andrew Probert designed them as vampire-like aliens with triangular heads that were far more menacing than what appeared in "The Last Outpost." They seemed more like the Jerry Lewises of the galaxy than Dr. Lectors or Freddy Kruegers. (The eventual effective villains, the Borgs, owed a bit to the implacable Terminator, exploiting the fears of dehumanization via cybernetics or biomechanical synthesis.)

RECURRING CHARACTERS

Both shows soon found their stride, though NEXT GENERATION improved in its third year while Trek Classic started downhill in that season. The place where NEXT GENERATION truly outdoes Trek Classic is with its continuing characters.

The original Trek had such recurring figures as the lovable rogue Harry Mudd. There was also Grace Lee Whitney's Yeoman Rand (a potential distraction for randy Captain Kirk, but a capable staff member nevertheless) and the too little seen Lt. Kevin Riley.

NEXT GENERATION has John deLancie's delightful Q (a clear variation on Trelane, the omnipotent, tormenting child from Trek Classic's "Squire of Gothos," but given its own personal spin by deLancie's characterization. Majel Barrett's insufferable Lwaxana Troi is an annoying Auntie Mame of the galaxy who only shined in "Half A Life" where her overbearing qualities were toned down a bit. Colm Meaney's appealing Chief O'Brien, the fan response to which helped bring him forward until he finally received a co-starring role on DEEP SPACE NINE.

Guinan, the seemingly omniscient bartender counsels but isn't telling all her secrets, and who through Whoopi Goldberg's winning performance helps throw key issues into clear relief. She seems particularly reticent to share information about the Q and the Borg even when such information could be vital.

Vash (Jennifer Hetrick), who vamps Picard to such an extent that the usually clearheaded commander can seem befuddled. The delightful screw-up Lt. Barclay (Dwight Schultz), an endearing wannabe with human failings and fantasies. Worf's lively ex-girlfriend K'Ehleyr (Suzie Plakson) who unfortunately was killed off in "Reunion," and a few others who have made brief but vivid impressions during their encounters with the Enterprise crew.

PLUNDERED IDEAS

While Trek Classic was maybe too fond of stories where Kirk encounters a screwed-up culture and does something altering the circumstances to fix it, NEXT GENERATION gets into similar ruts. How many stories have there been where some mysterious alien tortures one of the crew members? Or where one of the crew (or all of the crew) gets amnesia and has to piece together what has happened? Or the Enterprise encounters a powerful alien that threatens to destroy the Enterprise only to escape and never communicate with this new (albeit dangerous) lifeform?

And indeed, the first season of NEXT GENERATION was rife with episodes rewriting concepts that appeared in Trek Classic and not doing them as well, beginning with "Encounter at Farpoint" which borrowed elements of "The Changeling" and "Squire of Gothos" to disappointing effect. "The Naked Now" was supposed to flesh out the characters the way "Naked Time" has revealed hidden aspects of the Trek

Classic characters, but instead the women all got horny and the men acted drunk.

"Where No One Has Gone Before" revamped an idea from the Trek novel THE WOUNDED SKY (by Diane Duane) but handled it nowhere nearly as well. "Lonely Among Us" was a tiresome, ineptly humorous retread of "Journey To Babel," and "Datalore" resurrected the awful evil twin cliché. "Home Soil" was a particularly poor rewrite of "Devil in the Dark" as "The Neutral Zone" was a poor variation on "Space Seed," both of which Trek Classic obviously did much better.

NEXT GENERATION has been consistently poor in trying to present monsters or scares. The ineffective episodes "The Child" and "Devil's Due" were both resurrected from the proposed but unfilmed STAR TREK II series Paramount had planned in 1977 but then scrapped in favor of STAR TREK: THE MOTION PICTURE.

"Unnatural Selection" didn't grip the way "The Deadly Years" did, while its solution was lifted from the animated STAR TREK episode "Counter-Clock Incident" and suggests that a character could be resurrected in the Transporter at any time.

THE BAD WITH THE GOOD

Both series had their share of bad episodes, Trek Classic's being the infamous "And The Children Shall Lead," "Spock's Brain" (a comedy played as if it were to be taken seriously with most of the jokes cut out), the scientifically inept "Wink Of An Eye," the awful hippie stereotypes of "Way To Eden" and the overbearing patriotism of "The Omega Glory" (which is also another parallel Earth culture story).

NEXT GENERATION can choose among "The Royale," a lost in limbo episode which should have stayed that way. "Up The Long Ladder" which resurrects awful stereotypes about Irishmen and puts them into the 24th century intact. "Samaritan Snare," a sort of "morons in outer space" that left more than Geordi exasperated. "Menage A Trois" with Lwaxana at her worst and a horny Ferengi after her. "Shades of Gray," the cost-saving, pointless clip show, and "Angel One." The most sexist Trek show since "Turnabout Intruder" suggested that women simply weren't capable of being starship captains.

However, the reason we remember and honor both series is for their finest endeavors, not their worst, and both series have an ample supply of these. Both series not only give hope by showing the human adventure continuing, but they also bring into homes across the planet ideas of what humankind has achieved and can achieve. In dealing with the problems of being a Vulcan in Trek Classic or exploring the alienness of Klingon culture or trying to fit in as a human when one is an android in NEXT GENERATION, both Trek series offer new perspectives to look at age-old human questions.

Whichever approach one prefers, both have clearly shown that at their best they have much to offer the intelligent viewer for both Trek shows have gambled on their audience's intelligence and won a wide following for respecting it. We can only hope that future science fiction and drama shows can follow their proud example.

WILLIAM SHATNER AT THE 25TH ANNIVERSARY OF STAR TREK CELEBRATION.

THE MAN WHO CREATED STAR TREK: GENE RODDENBERRY

James Van Hise

The complete life story of the man who created STAR TREK, reveals the man and his work.

$14.95 in stores ONLY $12.95 to Couch Potato Catalog Customers
160 Pages
ISBN # 1-55698-318-2

TWENTY-FIFTH ANNIVERSARY TREK TRIBUTE

James Van Hise

Taking a close up look at the amazing Star Trek stroy, this book traces the history of the show that has become an enduring legend. James Van Hise chronicles the series from 1966 to its cancellation in 1969, through the years when only the fans kept it alive, and on to its unprecedented revival. He offers a look at its latter-day blossoming into an animated series, a sequence of five movies (with a sixth in preparation) that has grossed over $700 million, and the offshoot "The Next Generation" TV series.

The author gives readers a tour of the memorials at the Smithsonian and the Movieland Wax Museums, lets them witness Leonard Nimoy get his star on the Hollywood Walk Of Fame in 1985, and takes them behind the scenes of the motion-picture series and TV's "The Next Generation." The concluding section examines the future of Star Trek beyond its 25th Anniversary.

$14.95.....196 Pages
ISBN # 1-55698-290-9

THE HISTORY OF TREK
James Van Hise

The complete story of Star Trek from Original conception to its effects on millions of Lives across the world. This book celebrates the 25th anniversary of the first "Star Trek" television episode and traces the history of the show that has become an enduring legend—even the non-Trekkies can quote specific lines and characters from the original television series. The History of Trek chronicles "Star Trek" from its start in 1966 to its cancellation in 1969; discusses the lean years when "Star Trek" wasn't shown on television but legions of die hard fans kept interest in it still alive; covers the sequence of five successful movies (and includes the upcoming sixth one); and reviews "The Next Generation" television series, now entering its sixth season. Complete with Photographs, The History of Trek reveals the origins of the first series in interviews with the original cast and creative staff. It also takes readers behind the scenes of all six Star Trek movies, offers a wealth of Star Trek Trivia, and speculates on what the future may hold.

$14.95.....160 Pages
ISBN # 1-55698-309-3

THE MAN BETWEEN THE EARS:
STAR TREKS LEONARD NIMOY
James Van Hise

Based on his numerous interviews with Leonard Nimoy, Van Hise tells the story of the man as well as the entertainer.

This book chronicles the many talents of Leonard Nimoy from the beginning of his career in Boston to his latest starring work in the movie, Never Forget. His 25-year association with Star Trek is the centerpiece, but his work outside the Starship Enterprise is also covered, from such early efforts as Zombies of the Stratosphere to his latest directorial and acting work, and his stage debut in Vermont.

$14.95.....160 Pages
ISBN # 1-55698-304-2

COUCH POTATO INC.   5715 N. Balsam Rd   Las Vegas, NV 89130   (702)658-2090

Use Your Credit Card 24 HRS — Order toll Free From: **(800)444-2524** Ext 67

TREK: THE MAKING OF THE MOVIES

James Van Hise

TREK: THE MAKING OF THE MOVIES tells the complete story both on-screen and behind the scenes of the biggest STAR TREK adventures of all. Plus the story of the STAR TREK II that never happened and the aborted STAR TREK VI: STARFLEET ACADEMY.

$14.95.....160 Pages
ISBN # 1-55698-313-1

TREK: THE LOST YEARS

Edward Gross

The tumultouos, behind-the-scenes saga of this modern day myth between the cancellation of the original series in 1969 and the announcement of the first movie ten years later. In addition, the text explores the scripts and treatments written throughout the 1970's, including every proposed theatrical feature and an episode guide for STAR TREK II, with comments from the writers whose efforts would ultimately never reach the screen.

This volume came together after years of research, wherein the author interviewed a wide variety of people involved with every aborted attempt at revival, from story editors to production designers to David Gautreaux, the actor signed to replace Leonard Nimoy; and had access to exclusive resource material, including memos and correspondences, as well as teleplays and script outlines.

$12.95.....132 Pages
ISBN # 1-55698-220-8

COUCH POTATO INC.   5715 N. Balsam Rd   Las Vegas, NV 89130   (702)658-2090

Use Your Credit Card 24 HRS — Order toll Free From: **(800)444-2524** Ext 67